d | e | w | e | y

COLOR SYSTEM ™

EMBRAC**E**
HU**E**
YOU
ARE™

DEWEY SADKA

The Dewey Color System™
Embrace Hue You Are
(First Edition)
by Dewey Sadka
© Copyright 2001 Energia,® Inc.
Patent Pending

Not for release.
The Dewey Color System™
Embrace Hue You Are
by Dewey Sadka

Copyright © 2001 by Energia,® Inc.
PRINTED IN THE UNITED STATES OF AMERICA
Energia,® Inc. The Dewey Color System™ First Edition
1.****2.*******3.********
4.****5.*******6.********

Library of Congress Catalog
Card Number 99-094838
ISBN No. 0-9671207-0-5 Soft-cover

This book is dedicated to my mother,
Louise Moses Sadka,
for teaching me to think,
and to everyone
who is seeking to increase
their passion for life
or support those they love.

CONTENTS

A NOTE FROM THE AUTHOR - - - - - - - - - - - - - - - - -11

1 THE SCIENCE OF COLOR
   beyond language -13
   the concept -14

2 THE DEWEY COLOR SYSTEM™
   a reliable system -15
   a brief historical perspective - - - - - - - - - - - - - - - - - -16
   a model was adopted -17
   frequently asked questions - - - - - - - - - - - - - - - - - - -20

3 CHOOSE YOUR COLORS
   get ready! -21
   primary & secondary category - - - - - - - - - - - - - - - - -22
   achromatic & intermediate category - - - - - - - - - - - - -23
   my color category page -25
   mental shades -26
   physical shades -27
   spiritual shades -28
   silent shades -29
   my color shades page -31

4   USING YOUR NEW LANGUAGE

a major breakthrough -33
get to know yourself -34
learn about friends and loved ones - - - - - - - - - - - - - - -34
teach your children -35
revitalize your home -35
enhance your wardrobe -35

5   YOUR BASIC MOTIVATORS

yellow: realistic, diplomatic, giving - - - - - - - - - - - - - - -39
blue: planner, initiator, visionary - - - - - - - - - - - - - - - - -43
red: practical, resourceful, direct - - - - - - - - - - - - - - - - -47
where do you fit in? -51
me and you -53
your primary focus -56
how color language evolved - - - - - - - - - - - - - - - - - - -58
primary iq -59

6   HOW YOU RELATE

green: nurturing, concerned, comfortable - - - - - - - - - - -63
purple: determined, dramatic, empowering - - - - - - - - - -67
orange: bold, sentimental, dedicated - - - - - - - - - - - - - -71
finding your niche -75
getting in sync -77
your secondary connection -79
how color language evolved - - - - - - - - - - - - - - - - - - -81
secondary iq -82

7   WHO YOU ARE

yellow and green - the caretakers - - - - - - - - - - - - - - - -87
yellow and purple - the catalysts - - - - - - - - - - - - - - - -89
yellow and orange - the technical thinkers - - - - - - - - - -91
blue and green - the anchors - - - - - - - - - - - - - - - - - - -93
blue and purple - the thinkers - - - - - - - - - - - - - - - - - -95

blue and orange - the builders - - - - - - - - - - - - - - - - - -97
red and green - the resource managers - - - - - - - - - - - -99
red and purple - the synthesizers - - - - - - - - - - - - - - -101
red and orange - the humanitarians - - - - - - - - - - - - -103
identify your role model - - - - - - - - - - - - - - - - - - -104

8 YOUR HOPES AND FEARS

black: emotional, focused, loyal - - - - - - - - - - - - - - -107
white: objective, curious, analytical - - - - - - - - - - - - -111
brown: aware, authentic, compassionate - - - - - - - - - -115
predicting outcomes -119
sexual chemistry -121
your achromatic boundaries - - - - - - - - - - - - - - - - - -124
how color language evolved - - - - - - - - - - - - - - - - - -126
achromatic iq -127

9 YOUR ENERGY TYPE

yellow, green and black - the truth seekers - - - - - - - - -130
yellow, green and white - the designers - - - - - - - - - - -132
yellow, green and brown - the givers - - - - - - - - - - - - -134
yellow, purple and black - the facilitators - - - - - - - - - -136
yellow, purple and white - the spiritual wizards - - - - - - -138
yellow, purple and brown - the shamans - - - - - - - - - - -140
yellow, orange and black - the inventors - - - - - - - - - - -142
yellow, orange and white - the information junkies - - - - -144
yellow, orange and brown - the troubleshooters - - - - - - -146
blue, green and black - the identity creators - - - - - - - - -148
blue, green and white - the intellectuals - - - - - - - - - - -150
blue, green and brown - the dream makers - - - - - - - - -152
blue, purple and black - the pioneers - - - - - - - - - - - - -154
blue, purple and white - the problem solvers - - - - - - - -156
blue, purple and brown - the scientific thinkers - - - - - - -158
blue, orange and black - the managers - - - - - - - - - - - -160
blue, orange and white - the social investigators - - - - - -162
blue, orange and brown - the activists - - - - - - - - - - - -164

red, green and black - the investors - - - - - - - - - - - - - -166
red, green and white - the practical wizards - - - - - - - - -168
red, green and brown - the crusaders - - - - - - - - - - - - -170
red, purple and black - the entertainers - - - - - - - - - - - -172
red, purple and white - the forecasters - - - - - - - - - - - -174
red, purple and brown - the generators - - - - - - - - - - - -176
red, orange and black - the consultants - - - - - - - - - - - -178
red, orange and white - the resource directors - - - - - - - -180
red, orange and brown - the inspectors - - - - - - - - - - - -182

10 TAKING ON THE WORLD
lime green: logical, self-investigative - - - - - - - - - - - - -187
magenta: enthusiastic, socially investigative - - - - - - - - -191
teal: social worth, empathy - - - - - - - - - - - - - - - - - - -195
red-orange: personal worth, self-respect - - - - - - - - - - -199
indigo: conceptual, self-confident - - - - - - - - - - - - - -203
gold: resourceful, playful -207
color commentary -210
how color language evolved - - - - - - - - - - - - - - - - - - -212
intermediate iq -213

11 HAPPINESS AND HEALING
the mental shades - achieving serenity - - - - - - - - - - - -217
the physical shades - maintaining positive relationships -223
the spiritual shades - accepting yourself - - - - - - - - - - -229
the silent shades - creating hope - - - - - - - - - - - - - - -235

12 COLOR SHOPPING GUIDE
become empowered -239
become a color expert -240
dewey color system™ -242
triadic combinations -245
color complements -248
split complements -250
take it shopping -257

13 COLOR COORDINATE YOU
    create a new you -261
    go ahead—be sexy! -262
    balance your upper and lower body - - - - - - - - - - - - -264
    create the perfect look -265
    the rows -269
    the columns -275
    why did you wear that color today? - - - - - - - - - - - - -279

14 COLOR YOUR WORLD
    aesthetics 101 -283
    the rows -285
    the columns -291

15 MUSCLE UP
    truth is simple -295
    the 15 great powers -297
    be true to yourself -329
    The Dewey Color System™ oath - - - - - - - - - - - - - - -331
    on a final note -332

    official color pages -333
    acknowledgments -338
    check out our web site -339
    Energia® Press -340

A NOTE FROM THE AUTHOR

Refining the talents of others has been my life's work. For over 18 years, as the director and owner of a large employee staffing company, I found it especially rewarding to look beyond the surface, to try to see the inner workings of each person.

By constantly encouraging my employees and clients to stress their heartfelt thoughts, I became aware of their feelings and needs. This allowed me to identify the things that motivated them. My efforts to make each one of them a winner made me a winner.

Since I believe that success occurs when people do what they enjoy, I began searching for a simple key to better understand the desires, concerns, different perspectives, and passions of those individuals who would determine my future.

My experiences with traditional personality evaluations were that they only scratched the surface of understanding an individual. I knew that if I could invent an evaluation that revealed the motivating factors of each person, productivity, sales, and employee morale would surely soar.

Ultimately, my unrelenting desire to know what makes me and those around me passionate led me to create The Dewey Color System™. My greatest wish is that this innovative method of using color to map your inner self will give you the self-knowledge to make your life passionate and fun.

THE SCIENCE OF COLOR

Color is a reflection of light. This reflection is what you see. It is received through the pupil of your eye in the form of varying wavelengths. This energy has a physical quality that each person reacts to differently. Even the blind have been able to identify specific colors, as verified in a study conducted by B.S. Sujendra Prakash.

Even though nothing inherently has a color, its reflection is interpreted by your brain as a distinguishable quality. Its vibration creates an unspoken energy. Yellow, for example, is widely considered to be irritating. Yet if you are a person who prefers yellow, you will find it inspirational, not irritating.

BEYOND LANGUAGE

Working in the staffing services business for over 24 years, I learned how thousands of people react during periods of crisis. After many years of observing others, I found that often I could predict people's actions and the eventual outcome of particular situations. This inspired me to look for patterns of human behavior that would tend to repeat themselves. My goal was to gain a more objective view of the needs of others and myself.

Chemistry and biology have physical structures that give them predictability. Biologists, for example, can analyze a blood cell and establish patterns that will tend to repeat under certain conditions. So why not seek to identify those patterns in human behavior as well?

the concept

The Dewey Color System™ is based on the concept that color can be used to reveal the core of an individual's personality. Concept-based theories have given the world its most far-reaching inventions. Here are a few:

★ "The earth is not the center of the universe."

-COPERNICUS

★ "Time stands still at the speed of light."

-ALBERT EINSTEIN

★ "A machine can think."

-ALBERT TOOLING

The Dewey Color System™ allows you to learn about yourself without feeling the pain of personally invasive questions. Don't let the fact that it's so easy discount the truth of this new system.

THE DEWEY COLOR SYSTEM™

The Dewey Color System™ uses color preference to show how each person prioritizes their life. Color preference is innate. A preferred color, for example, visually inspires a person to feel their hopes and aspirations. A non-preferred color irritatingly reminds them of what is missing in their life.

A RELIABLE SYSTEM

There are two ways we access knowledge—via concepts and experimentation. With the help of leading academic scholars, I put my concept to a rigorous test with well over 5,000 color profiles.

In a clinical comparison with America's leading personality evaluation systems, the Myers Briggs, the 16PF, and the Strong Interest Inventory, the following results were indicated.

★ 2 out of 3 participants believed that The Dewey Color System™ gave them a stronger awareness of themselves.

★ 3 out of 4 participants believed that The Dewey Color System™ better described how they live their lives.

"The Dewey Color System™ reliably measured color preferences." This was the conclusion of an additional study conducted by Edwin B. Hutchins, Ph.D. Dr. Hutchins has served as professor in the psychology department of several major universities and is well-known for his contributions to the field of medical education.

a brief historical perspective

Since the beginning of civilization, people have labored to discover the hidden motivations behind our actions. This effort has led to an abundance of systems that hold one thing in common: the endeavor to categorize and uncover the real person.

Early attempts to create a system of self-discovery led the curious to focus on external influences such as the stars, fate, or the elements. This gave rise to numerous systems that are still popular today.

Modern times, however, found investigators looking at the individual and free will. Gradually, empirical observation replaced even the most detailed systems of folklore and witchcraft, and in turn paved the way for psychology and the analysis of human behavior.

However, one thing has stymied all of these systems and those who administer them—the imprecision of language. Why? Simple. What happens, for example, if questions aren't asked properly? What if the people being questioned interpret them differently? What role does stress, fatigue, environment, prejudice, bias, and education play in the skewing of test results? Also, people frequently deceive themselves and fail to answer questions with complete honesty.

For all these reasons, experts have longed to create a language-free system to tell us about the individual.

the language of color

The solution to the problems of language-based tests was as simple as it was elegant. Color! How could anything be more obvious? Why not use color as an indicator of personality? No longer would there be a need to rely on words. Color could allow you to ask questions without words. The confusion of meanings and interpretation would be altogether eliminated.

a model was adopted

In 1981, I began searching for a physical structure that would lend predictability to personality. I adopted an atom of carbon as the model since it was the only element common to all living things. Below you can see two illustrated cross-sections of the carbon model used as the foundation of The Dewey Color System™. Black and brown form the magnetic poles. White, absorbed light, is the catalyst for change.

BLACK: THE MENTAL POLE

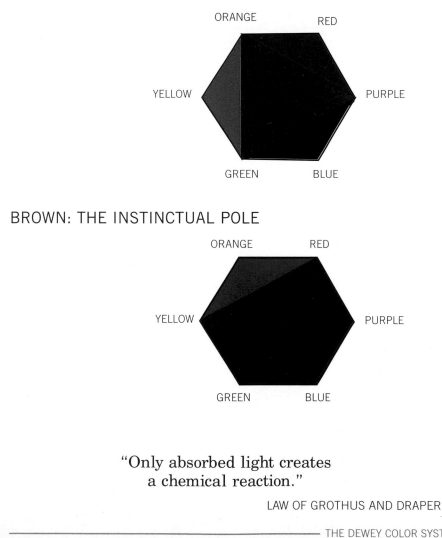

BROWN: THE INSTINCTUAL POLE

"Only absorbed light creates
a chemical reaction."

LAW OF GROTHUS AND DRAPER

color language evolved

Albert Einstein once said, "If you have a question about life, look to nature." So I did just what Albert told me to do. I looked to nature. I investigated the apparent functions of each color in nature to give it language—a verbal meaning. For example, green only exists where there is fertile soil. Isn't this the essence of nurturing? Visit the language evolution of each color at the end of chapters 5, 6, 8, and 10 to better understand your essence.

a language web created 51 colors

Nature's way of creating color expanded the "language web" of the system. For example, two primaries, blue and yellow, combine to make a secondary, green. A primary and a secondary, blue and green, combine to make an intermediate, teal.

Logic further extended the language in the system. Blue, for example, is initiating a dream. Yellow is awareness of others' perspectives. Together they create green, the awareness of how to create a fertile soil to initiate a dream.

Each color represents a personal value you need to honor. Your color selection reveals the rewards and consequences of how you prioritize your life. There are 3,375 color combinations in The Dewey Color System™.

AS YOU CONTINUE TO EXPLORE YOUR COLOR PREFERENCES, KEEP IN MIND THAT YOUR PERSONALITY REFLECTS A COMBINATION OF COLORS, NOT JUST ONE.

connect with the system

In the next chapter you will be asked to select your color choices from the Primary, Secondary, Achromatic, Intermediate, and Color Shade categories.

Examine the illustration below as a frame of reference to view what each category will reveal within you. The deepest part of you is reflected in your achromatic selection. The part of you that is most apparent to others is expressed by your intermediate selection. As you read keep in mind that each layer within you acts autonomously, as if the others didn't exist.

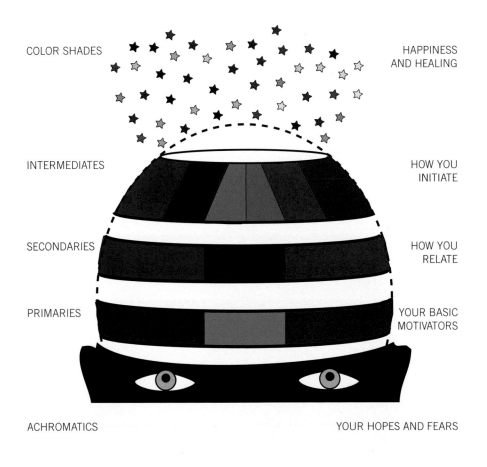

COLOR SHADES   HAPPINESS AND HEALING

INTERMEDIATES   HOW YOU INITIATE

SECONDARIES   HOW YOU RELATE

PRIMARIES   YOUR BASIC MOTIVATORS

ACHROMATICS   YOUR HOPES AND FEARS

FREQUENTLY ASKED QUESTIONS

can i make a mistake?

It's unlikely that you'll choose a color that's not meant for you. How can you not choose what you already instinctively know? However, if the personality descriptions based on the colors you initially choose seem to be off the mark, read about the other colors and see which apply the most to you. Then, choose your colors again. Could it be that you are avoiding your basic self?

If you have a strong reaction to the color description, good or bad, you've probably picked the right color. You'll tend to feel indifference when reading about your incorrect colors. If you're someone who works with colors a lot, such as a painter or graphic designer, it can be especially difficult to make your selection.

If you feel that you are not that way any more, your colors might be showing your core personality responses, not your actions. Training and experience have taught you lessons that allow you to change the way you act. Get upset, though, and you'll need to struggle to keep this core part of you from taking over.

what if i'm color-blind?

The system is still functional. It will just take you longer to make your choices. So, take your time. Generally, you will dislike the colors you cannot see. You will have an emotional need to learn and express what these color areas represent.

will my colors change?

You bet! When your life changes, so can your colors. Leaving home, getting married, having children, losing someone close to you—all of these events can change your color preferences. For the most part, however, your colors change in varying degrees and not as dramatically as you might think.

If your color choices change, read about your new colors in the color change paragraph at the end of chapters 5, 6, 8, and 10. You will gain insight into your current needs.

3 chapter

CHOOSE YOUR COLORS

You are about to begin a quest that will deepen your understanding of yourself and intensify your passion for life. Be prepared to view a new yet somehow familiar perspective of who you are, what you do, and why you do it.

GET READY!

Find a place where you can choose your colors without being interrupted. A room with good white light, not yellow or blue, is appropriate, or look for a space with natural light.

You may find it helpful to keep a pen or pencil handy to make notes along the way.

Forget your favorite colors. Eliminate from your mind the colors you like to wear and decorate with.

Don't rush. Feel the colors. Let them pick you! There are no right or wrong, good or bad color choices—only your choices.

TURN TO THE NEXT 8 PAGES TO
MAKE YOUR COLOR SELECTIONS.

PRIMARY CATEGORY
Select your favorite and least favorite

YELLOW   BLUE   RED

SECONDARY CATEGORY
Select your favorite and least favorite

GREEN   PURPLE   ORANGE

ACHROMATIC CATEGORY
Select your favorite and least favorite

BLACK

WHITE

BROWN

INTERMEDIATE CATEGORY
Select your two favorites and two least favorites

| TEAL | MAGENTA | GOLD |
| RED-ORANGE | LIME GREEN | INDIGO |

COLOR NOTES

MY COLOR CATEGORY PAGE

Your color category selections:

CATEGORY	FAVORITE	LEAST FAVORITE
PRIMARY		
SECONDARY		
ACHROMATIC		
INTERMEDIATE		

★ Additional color pages on 333-337

MENTAL SHADES
Select your two favorites

SPRING GREEN	MINT GREEN	SEA GREEN	SKY BLUE

CAMEL	OLIVE	OCEAN BLUE	EARTH

PALM GREEN	EMERALD	FOREST GREEN	NAVY

PHYSICAL SHADES
Select your two favorites

PERIWINKLE

LAVENDER

ORCHID

PINK

SIENNA

GRAPE

GARNET

APPLE RED

COBALT   DARK PURPLE   MULBERRY   CRANBERRY

SPIRITUAL SHADES
Select your two favorites

SALMON

APRICOT

GOLDEN

PALE YELLOW

WARM RED

CLAYPOT

BRONZE

MUSTARD

RUBY

MAHOGANY

LEAF

MOSS

SILENT SHADES
Select your two favorites

PEWTER	DESERT	ALMOND

GRAY	TAN	BEIGE

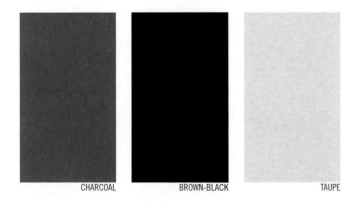

CHARCOAL	BROWN-BLACK	TAUPE

COLOR NOTES

MY COLOR SHADES PAGE
Your color shades selections:

SHADE	1ST FAVORITE	2ND FAVORITE
MENTAL		
PHYSICAL		
SPIRITUAL		
SILENT		

★ Additional color pages on 333-337

WHAT YOUR CHOICES REPRESENT

Each of these color categories represents different aspects of your personality: motivation, hidden agendas, fears, temperament, perception, coping mechanisms, interpersonal skills, strengths, weaknesses, hopes, and ambitions.

YOUR FAVORITE COLORS REPRESENT YOUR HOPES AND ASPIRATIONS, THE IDEALS YOU PURSUE WITH PASSION. The more you accept this passionate part of yourself, the more successful you will be. These colors also reveal the difficulties you experience when you make your passions your only priority.

YOUR LEAST FAVORITE COLORS ARE AS SIGNIFICANT AS YOUR FAVORITE COLORS. THEY HIGHLIGHT THE ISSUES AND EXPERIENCES THAT YOU TRY TO AVOID FACING. Dealing with what you would normally avoid is essential to your personal growth. It allows you to better manage your life.

YOUR FAVORITE AND LEAST FAVORITE SELECTIONS WILL REVEAL THE TWIN FORCES IN YOUR LIFE. In gaining a greater awareness of your personality, passions, and power, you'll acquire the knowledge to create positive change without destroying your essence.

"You cannot separate the good from the bad and perhaps there is no need to do so."

JACQUELINE KENNEDY ONASSIS

4

USING YOUR NEW LANGUAGE

Use the color interpretations in The Dewey Color System™ to embrace the passions within yourself, to respect the motivations of those you love, and to electrify your life by creating a more colorful wardrobe and home decor. You will gain the courage and confidence to do what you do best.

A MAJOR BREAKTHROUGH

Imagine a system so understandable and so much fun that even a child could use it. It would be nothing short of revolutionary. Well, here you have it.

This is the first evaluation system to extensively use color preference to bypass language. Instead of relying on lengthy, imprecise questionnaires, The Dewey Color System™ uses a simple, highly accurate methodology based on your color preferences to reveal who you are—not who you believe yourself to be.

The Dewey Color System™ is the first to recognize the connection between personality and the four distinct color categories: Primary Colors, Secondary Colors, Achromatic Colors, and Intermediate Colors. It incorporates employee evaluation systems, once only available to the professional community, and turns them into a valuable new test accessible to the public. After reading The Dewey Color System™ you will find hundreds of uses for it in your everyday life.

USE #1: GET TO KNOW YOURSELF

Too many of us wander through life with uncertainty and a lack of clarity. It's the unknown, the incomprehensible that leads to fear, resentment, loneliness, failure, and even poverty. Once you understand yourself, everything begins to flow: love, wisdom, strength, prosperity, happiness, and serenity.

Your life today is richer because color was used to indicate chemical reactions in science and medicine. The Dewey Color System™ takes you beyond these established uses of color. By focusing on your preferences for precise shades of color, the system will indicate who you are and how you relate to others, make decisions, solve problems, and approach the world.

USE #2: LEARN ABOUT FRIENDS AND LOVED ONES

Reading The Dewey Color System™ with those closest to you will allow you to see what is special about you and your relationships. Discovering your friends' and loved ones' talents will help you understand why they are so important in your life. When you comprehend their fears, you will have more patience to help them in times of crisis. We have provided space at the back of the book for you to record the colors of friends and loved ones.

Which colors do your friends and loved ones prefer? What about those people you argue with or dislike? Find out how you interact with different "color types" and how to make the best out of your relationships. Your life will never be the same.

USE #3: TEACH YOUR CHILDREN

Children are great with colors. Not nearly as bewildered by choice as adults, they select their colors quickly and with remarkable self-assuredness. Adult experiences form layers of facts and agendas that interfere with our ability to see clearly.

If you have young children, translate the meaning of their color choices for them. They will discover tremendous personal insights and develop a strong sense of self-esteem. By understanding their passions, you'll gain the power to better support them without destroying their essence.

USE #4: REVITALIZE YOUR HOME

You'll learn how to create a more supportive environment and decorate a room so that you feel good about yourself. Color can give you the impetus to become more spiritual, more adventurous, and even more sensual. You will learn color combinations that will make your rooms—and you—come alive. Color has the power to transform your space into a sacred place.

USE #5: ENHANCE YOUR WARDROBE

Before you start on your shopping adventure, use these 6,000-plus sizzling, snazzy, and sensible color combinations to make what you already own more exciting. Then take this book shopping and color coordinate a new you. Tell the world who you are.

DON'T BE IN A RUSH! IF YOU READ THIS BOOK TOO QUICKLY, YOU WON'T BE ABLE TO ABSORB EVERYTHING IT HAS TO OFFER. SO RELAX AND GET READY TO TAKE A PASSIONATE JOURNEY INSIDE YOURSELF.

5 chapter

YOUR BASIC MOTIVATORS

Yellow, blue, and red are the main sources of your energy–the fuel in your engine. The primary colors indicate in the broadest sense who you are. The directness of these strong hues can be energizing or imposing. Before you begin, select your primary colors from page 22.

IN THIS CHAPTER

CONCENTRATE ON UNDERSTANDING THE MOTIVATIONAL FORCES WITHIN YOU. You will be able to tap your passions and channel them toward making your life more enjoyable and meaningful.

YOUR FAVORITE PRIMARY COLOR determines how you attack life. It indicates what you feel you need to accomplish to be yourself.

YOUR LEAST FAVORITE PRIMARY COLOR, on the other hand, determines what you try to avoid and emotionally suppress. In confronting these concerns you gain the power to stay on track and not let incidental things distract you from your goals.

PRIMARY COLORS ENERGIZE

The primary colors are the source of all other colors. Respecting your favorite and least favorite choices will give you the power to fire up your engine and stay focused on your main goals in life. Prioritizing the rewarding areas of your life will maintain your steam and vigor. Obstacles will become insignificant details.

PRIMARY NOTES

> "Knowledge is power."
>
> FRANCIS BACON

yellow

beyond words

Finding common ground is the game you play best. You calm troubled situations, bridge differences. Your awareness of others' perspectives allows you to express contrary, unpopular feelings without offending anyone. By keeping people listening, you allow solutions and possibilities to unfold.

In one-on-one situations you manage to see and understand the other person's point of view. You accept what others need without imposing your own will or agenda. You accept people for who they are. You have a knack for keeping the conversation flowing and know precisely where to focus your energy. In groups you keep to yourself; unlike the blues, you keep your energy.

You're a team player and enjoy the supportive role, for example, the person behind the president. You are flexible. Since you are not a control freak or power hungry, you're able to focus on the task at hand. You deal with the present and don't dwell on the past or obsessively plan for the future. You tend to be spiritual and life-supporting.

key words
REALISTIC
DIPLOMATIC
GIVING

power
WISDOM TO KNOW
WHAT IS NEEDED

motivation
PERSONAL GROWTH

the lovable you

You enjoy the simple pleasures in life and you give this gift to your relationships as well. You are at your best when those around you are not judgmental or impatient. Rigidity turns you off. Others turn you on when they refrain from speaking until all the facts are presented.

You're very generous, willing to extend yourself without expecting anything in return. However, you find it difficult to receive. You end up feeling less together-as if you should have done it for yourself. The people closest to you find it hard to do something special for you.

Allow for give and take. You make others feel important when you let them be there for you. It is advisable to show others your weaknesses; otherwise, you'll find yourself surrounded by people who take advantage of you.

setting priorities

Your ability to understand everyone else's point of view is a very powerful tool in the workplace. Knowing how to approach a potential client and getting the boss to listen to a new idea are among your natural talents. Unlike the reds, you are seldom too direct.

You have the power to establish new relationships and move up the corporate ladder. People feel they know where they stand with you, and are willing to let you help them. You are happy when you're able to give of yourself.

For you, success means growing and learning. You're not overly concerned with money. You would much rather be in a position that gives you a good feeling about yourself than work at a job you hate, but which pays more. Be careful. You can become too absorbed with the different facets of projects. Constantly remind yourself of the larger picture.

do it right

You have the power to take in the beauty that surrounds you and really appreciate everything that life has to offer. Being an integral part of the world is the source of all your energy. You achieve personal growth and enjoy the process of living when absorbed in a task. You are at your best when shopping or relaxing.

don't go there

When you do things for others to avoid dealing with your own needs, you don't give yourself the time or the energy to think about your own dilemmas. The more upset you become, the more you immerse yourself in the concerns of others. In turn, you become overly docile and unable to help yourself. Your problems, of course, will not go away until you confront them.

create passion

Discover those places that allow your fluid, easygoing charm to resonate with people. Avoid overly structured, repressive environments.

yellow

YOU ARE VERY DETERMINED

When you really want something, others had better get out of your way. Your sense of responsibility and urgency keeps those around you moving forward. You create a sense of purpose. You are constantly thinking, "I must do this or that." Your mind is one step ahead of everyone else's. You're on automatic pilot. This gives you the power to persuade those around you to believe in your way of doing things. After all, you look as if you know what you want, even when you're not sure.

The friends and lovers in your life sometimes take a back seat to whatever project you're involved with. But once you meet someone you're really interested in, you obsess over him or her. You want it all and you want it now. Don't be so forceful. Accept people for who they are, not who you want them to be. If you stop trying to change people, they will be better able to love you back.

At work, you are exceptionally goal-oriented and have a clear idea of the objective at hand. If things take too long, you become impatient. You have a steady need to complete something. Your first thought is, "Why isn't this finished already?" When your sense of urgency is overwhelming, you can send destructive messages. Others can see you as a person who cares only about the bottom line and not people. You can end up doing things twice because you are sometimes in too much of a rush.

Slow down, enjoy the process of living. Before you start something new, take the time to appreciate the important things you have already accomplished. You will feel more connected to the world and less isolated. Achieving things is not the only measure of success. Recognize that learning something is reason enough to feel good about yourself.

> ## "I dream my painting and then paint my dream."
>
> VINCENT VAN GOGH

blue

beyond words

You are a dreamer and a visionary—wistful, imaginative, and eccentric. You're preoccupied with the future. Your dreams give you the mental discipline to concentrate and stay on track. You need to justify your life by making a positive impact on the world, even on those you don't know.

Thinking about the future energizes you. Putting forth your ideas and reshaping the world are key to your happiness. You are seeking a more cohesive world. Making sure that everyone is on the same page is a major concern. You need agreement to initiate positive change.

You require recognition. The most idealistic of all the colors, you are often distracted by your own schemes. Mood swings have you feeling depressed one day and euphoric the next. Too much validation from others can make you conceited. Too little can make you depressed.

key words
PLANNER
INITIATOR
VISIONARY

power
ABILITY TO VISUALIZE
THE FUTURE

motivation
TO JUSTIFY YOUR
EXISTENCE

the lovable you

You see the sunny side of each person. Putting others on a pedestal makes you feel good about yourself. But be careful. It's vital that your judgment be realistic. Growth in relationships can only be achieved when you perceive things clearly and entirely. Learn to view the negative in conjunction with the positive. Every person has both.

When you first meet someone, appearance is everything. Don't be naive. If you assume that people are who they say they are, you can be vulnerable to con artists. Make sure you appraise people by their actions, not by their words. This will keep you from getting burned. You are especially susceptible to flattery. If you feel someone needs to change or are repeatedly being burned, be cautious. Set boundaries that protect you. Keep your power. Don't allow someone to get too close until you see beyond appearances.

setting priorities

Your ability to visualize helps you be proactive. Blues can fix things before they are broken! When you enjoy your work, you become tenacious about achieving your objective. This sends the message to those around you that you are in total control. You can pull together a team. Isn't that the formula for a successful beginning?

You need to work for a company where you are appreciated. When you are admired for your contributions, you believe in yourself. You gain the confidence to see the big picture of what the company needs or to develop something original.

Changes in your goals can create an identity crisis. You can become so attached to your goals, that you ignore good advice from others. Question those that disagree. Ask them their concerns. Loosen up. The end result will be even better than you originally envisioned.

do it right

When you focus on achieving your dreams, your ideas become so clear in your mind that you can easily see them happening. This gives you the knowledge to be successful and the confidence to believe in your goals. Others can assume you will succeed, even when you aren't sure what to do. You have the power to create images of a bright future for yourself and others.

don't go there

You tend to be too rigid and see things as right or wrong, this way or that. Your need to justify why someone disagrees with you makes it hard for you to see other people's perspectives. Reality won't live up to your expectations. Get with it. Allow others to exist as they are without any need to include or exclude them. Otherwise, your false perceptions will continue to make your life difficult. Others can see you as esoteric, even weird, if you become too preoccupied with your thoughts.

create passion

Accept others and situations as they are, even when they're not what you expected. You will become content with yourself and better able to create a successful future.

YOU ARE A FAIR CRITIC

You see different ways of deciphering situations, even when it is not acceptable to do so. You know how to categorize and identify what's most helpful. Since you're such a fair critic, you're a natural at setting standards and judging people and performances. Your talent lies in assessing the contributions of others.

You often model yourself after someone you admire and maintain a sharp lookout for a new guru or a new concept that you can dive into completely. When you become truly enthusiastic, you tend to lose yourself in your interests. You become the characters in the book you're reading or on your favorite television show. Since you often adopt new ideas and behaviors, sometimes you appear trendy.

Strong commitments are difficult for you. It's a real task "getting you to the altar." You find it difficult to put your faith in something that you can't clearly see. Your friends and lovers are often similar to you. They make you feel more together. Dressing like them, or making sure they dress a certain way, can also be a way of feeling closer together. At times, however, you make others feel rejected because they are different from you.

At work, your attention to detail allows you to juggle many tasks. However, you have a tendency to withhold information, sometimes even hiding facts from yourself. This gives those around you the perception that the situation is under control and that your goals are the same as theirs, even when they're not.

You talk to yourself a lot in an attempt to integrate your rational and emotional sides. Respect both aspects of your personality. There's room for compromise. Stay focused on your main objective, and don't get distracted by other issues. Your increased mental discipline will help you see the big picture, and you'll be better able to plan your future.

> "Do what you can, with what you have, where you are."
>
> THEODORE ROOSEVELT

red

beyond words

You know exactly what you want. Money, power, and status give you a sense of security but ultimately you use them as a means of expression. This is your primary goal. You're not one to hoard your wealth. On the contrary, you would give the shirt off your back for those you're concerned about.

You are ambitious, driven, confident, and outgoing. Red is a demanding, controlling color. It's also a practical color. You don't want to remake the world in your own image, like the blues. You just want to be in charge of fixing things. You have little tolerance for inefficiencies.

Even though your expressive style can make you appear extravagant, you are conservative. You learn what you need from past experiences. You are more realistic than someone who likes blue, because you have less need for validation and have a stronger sense of your own worth.

key words
PRACTICAL
RESOURCEFUL
DIRECT

power
USE EXPERIENCE
TO IMPROVE THINGS

motivation
TO BETTER
CONTROL YOUR
WORLD

red

the lovable you

You know exactly who you are and what you want. You believe that you do not exist until you express yourself, and it is common for you to state your opinions boldly. You feel complete when you're clear about where you stand. Your concern for the key people in your life gives you the power to focus on what you need to do.

You need physical contact to feel important. When you're having fun, you act like a fourteen-year-old. You make lots of noise and talk about what others are doing. This is especially true with friends who also like red. You tell stories about your experiences.

When you are comfortable in your environment, you're so outgoing and confident that everyone knows you exist. If you are a woman, however, you can be viewed as too strong. Since in many cultures women are judged by the way they enter the conversation, your outgoingness can be seen as too direct, or as an unacceptable role for a woman. So if you are a woman who likes red, be aware of what is and is not considered acceptable. Then, choose your direction and express yourself tactfully. It's OK if some men see you as difficult. Just make sure that the man you commit to accepts you for who you are. Otherwise, his ego can hinder you from expressing yourself, or you may run him off with your bossiness.

setting priorities

Your practical approach allows you to evaluate things and the people around you. You perform best when you are acting in the best interest of others. Your thinking is consistent and very factual. You help others around you recognize the facts and let them know when they are not being practical. Your opinions and observations correct their focus. You are motivated by the opportunity to direct others.

Money is important to you. You need to know if you're going to get your share. After all, money is recognition of a job well done and it shows that you are important. The accumulation of resources is your way of proving your self-worth. You believe strongly in getting it right the first time and are irritated when others leave promises unfulfilled. You have little patience with attitudes that reflect laziness or unwillingness to work. You believe rewards must be earned. If this attitude is carried too far, you can earn a reputation as a hard taskmaster. Others, though, will see you as a perfectionist.

do it right

Express yourself with sharp exuberance. You make things work better when you hold nothing back. Let your ideas and plans land with a big bang. You are at your best when shaking things up and getting things to work right. When others recognize that you have clear motives and expectations, they respect you or those you are protecting.

don't go there

You can be too direct and seek too much control of those around you. Others can see you as too conservative, limited, overly concerned with what has worked before and unwilling to look at what might work better. You become negative, too literal, and expect people to be as consistent and rational as you are. This can create an environment where positive change is difficult. At your worst, you are tyrannical. Too much power can corrupt you. You can lose sight of other people and be done in by your ego.

create passion

Temper your need to constantly evaluate situations and others' actions. You will see in detail what is working for you.

WHEN YOU SPEAK, OTHERS LISTEN

You analyze your thoughts before you speak. This gives you the ability to articulate how you feel with great depth. Therefore, when you speak, others listen. You can be impulsive. All of a sudden you're doing something you never could have imagined doing. These actions sometimes result in stories about you that you would not divulge to anyone. Your impulsive actions are manifestations of suppressed feelings and desires.

You are the confidant. Others trust you with their greatest secrets. You make them feel important. In fact, many times you hear more than you want to hear. When someone is telling you something that makes you feel uncomfortable, your face doesn't show a negative expression, even though your mind is thinking, "Help, why are they telling me this?" Therefore, they keep on talking. You hear details and stories that make soap operas sound boring.

With your friends and lovers, your hidden feelings create mystery. They make you sexy. Your curiosity, like a magnet, attracts the vulnerable part of others. After the relationship has started, others can become frustrated if you do not tell them what you need. As a child, did you feel that if you expressed how you felt, one of your parents wouldn't approve of you? Is your hesitation related to that fear? You must believe that when you express your needs to those who care about you, they will care even more.

At work, you occasionally forget to define what activities need to be done. This can make you a poor manager. Be firm. State each task, duty, or expectation in detail so that your co-workers know specifically what you want. Write things down. Then follow up.

When you don't initially speak up, others might see you as wimpy, weak, or politically neutral. Simply tell them, without emotion, "You will hear from me when I'm ready." They will then see that you have the tactical skills to say the appropriate things at the right time. This discovery will increase their respect for you.

WHERE DO YOU FIT IN?

COMBINE YOUR FAVORITE AND LEAST FAVORITE PRIMARY COLOR SELECTIONS TO SEE THE OVERALL, MOTIVATING POWER WITHIN YOU.

yellow favorite, red least favorite

You're the original "people person" with a flair for the social scene. A natural at public relations, you have the knack to see the other person's point of view without being judgmental. For that reason alone, people are willing to trust and confide in you. This provides you with the unvarnished facts needed to make decisions. Don't allow your support for others to interfere with your own future.

yellow favorite, blue least favorite

What some people and companies wouldn't give for you! You possess the uncanny ability to quickly grasp what those around you need. You can often locate the missing ingredient and turn what might have been a failure into a rousing success. Remain constantly aware of the big picture and don't get bogged down by any one task.

blue favorite, yellow least favorite

You are a wonderful strategist, able to plan future designs with a clear, sharp, and imaginative style. You love fantasy. However, while you may engage a plan with enthusiasm, what you think you want often differs from what you really need. Be more pragmatic, more sensible. Recognize that this isn't a perfect world. The faster you develop more realistic expectations, the more successful you will be.

blue favorite, red least favorite

You see the possibilities and limitations of your goals. This is a gift. You do not get angry if your future differs markedly from the way you envision it. You steadfastly hold on to your vision of where you want to go. Be mindful to clearly communicate all your expectations and wishes, or you may find you don't have the respect or support that you need.

red favorite, yellow least favorite

You are a perfectionist. More importantly, you know how to fix what isn't working. However, when overburdened, you have a tendency to see only the details or else skip the details entirely. Others may refer to you as rigid. Give yourself the chance to step back and reappraise things. There are many ways besides yours to accomplish a task.

red favorite, blue least favorite

You have the enviable talent to be able to appraise situations far better than those around you. Your ability to categorize things and estimate their value, however, can be lost in the specifics of a task. Staying focused on your overall objective will go a long way toward making you more successful. Don't let your concentration on the details sweep away your future.

ME AND YOU

IF YOUR FRIEND, PARTNER, OR CO-WORKER SELECTED...

THE SAME FAVORITE PRIMARY COLOR AS YOU, they give you the confidence to believe in yourself. They will motivate you.

A DIFFERENT FAVORITE PRIMARY COLOR THAN YOU, they allow you to see new possibilities. You will learn how to be more productive.

a yellow with a yellow

You allow each other to see your powers for being flexible. You create a world where conversations flow about the pleasant things in life. Your relationship is like a melody. Together you effortlessly attract others who give both of you new sources of stimulation. When you disagree, you simply change the subject. If this process is allowed to continue, your relationship is weakened.

a blue with a blue

You stay focused on the future. You talk about your plans. You see each other's wishes as if they were a reality. You encourage each other to "just do it." When you disagree, at first there is little to talk about. Both of you become stubborn. You both believe you are right. However, after your initial clash you usually compromise because both of you are uncomfortable with too much interpersonal conflict.

a red with a red

You constantly inspect things. You like to talk about everyone else. Marriages, dates, divorces, and sex are big topics. You want to hear about how others are living their lives. You both want to know all the details. You guessed it! You guys love gossip. It gives you new perspectives on how to live your own lives. If one of you dwells on his or her dilemma, the other will take over and become bossy. Then all hell breaks loose.

a yellow with a blue

You help each other stay focused on your relationships. As a yellow, you tell the blues when they are losing reality by becoming too linear. As a blue, you tell the yellows how to better determine where their relationship or situation is going. Together you're able to balance perspectives and ideas, keeping them relevant.

As a yellow, you teach blues how to understand different perspectives and to enjoy life. You teach them the art of flexibility. You also open the blue's world to new resources. By helping them to be more realistic about their expectations, you enable a blue to feel more like a winner. In a crisis you perceive blues as paying too much attention to their dreams, instead of to reality.

As a blue, you help the yellow better define their future. You turn their factual perspective into a structured plan. You admire the yellow's flexibility, yet become frustrated when you feel that goals aren't being met. You can see their flexibility as a sign of weakness or a lack of direction. The yellow then clashes with your authoritarianism. They feel you are jumping to conclusions too quickly instead of considering all the information available.

a yellow with a red

You can clearly define situations. As a yellow, you put a quick end to the red's love of gossip. As a red, you keep the yellow focused on how to accomplish their goals. This helps the yellow become more reliable.

As a yellow, you allow reds to see the limitations of their rules and agendas. You make them more flexible and better able to enjoy what they have and whom they are with. Reds are then able to relax and feel less confined. In a crisis, you see reds as too negative and overly structured.

As a red, you teach yellows how to be more specific and targeted on performance. The yellows love your ability to note detail. Too many rules, however, make the yellow feel confined. In a crisis, you fuel yellow's frustrations by bossing them around and failing to listen to their point of view.

a blue with a red

You can accomplish any task. As a blue, you help the reds believe that things can be better. Your dreams can make the red's tedious, task-oriented day go away. On the other hand, as a red, your eye for detail teaches the blues how to make things work. With your chop, chop, chop, you cut out what's not necessary. You make blue's ideas work.

As a blue, you constantly entertain the reds with your ideas. You encourage the more task-oriented reds to dream. By allowing the red to be less concerned with details, you open the red's eyes. You make looking forward to the future more fun. In a crisis, your ego may be wounded. You then discount the contributions of the red, dismissing their input as negative and nonconstructive.

As a red, you force the blues to express their needs more clearly. You coach them on how to pinpoint what they want so they can accomplish their ideas. By forcing the blue to face limitations, you help the blue to recognize that reworking is a normal part of life. When the blue ignores your input, you lose respect for the blue's creative contribution. You see them as incompetent, unaware of important details necessary to complete any creative endeavor.

YOUR PRIMARY FOCUS

IF YOU LIKE TWO PRIMARY CATEGORY COLORS EQUALLY, you can become confused about what to do next. You are pushing yourself to be more than you are right now. Others will see this pushy side of you as hard to understand. It's simply your way to gain clarity on what you want.

IF YOU PREFERRED THE COLORS IN THIS CATEGORY OVERALL, you are focused on your career. Your formal composure will make you appear to be a prince, princess, or a commander-in-chief. Discard your serious concerns and reveal your vulnerability or you will feel alone.

IF YOU DID NOT PREFER THE COLORS IN THIS CATEGORY OVERALL, you are going through a career crisis or avoiding doing what you really want to do. You might find the brightness of these colors a bit imposing or just too direct. Be more directive about your life. Recognize the consequences you are incurring by not being more specific about what you need to do.

laughing out loud

You will find yourself attracted to people who dislike the primary category colors you prefer. Your favorite selection will be the same as their least favorite. They naturally demonstrate the qualities you are striving to achieve. Sometimes, though, they really impose on your weakest, most uncomfortable area.

Those who have your same primary category colors are very confirming. They restore your faith in yourself. However, they can also be embarrassingly disturbing. Because they are so much like you, they also force you to see exactly who you are not. If you are really like one of your parents, or if one of your children is like you, you know this feeling well.

Let me share with you my favorite color, blue. When I talk with a person who dislikes blue, I discover that their point of view is distinctly different. Their questions force me to confront what I am most afraid to see. At times, I have even rejected their valuable perspective only to find out later that they were right on.

HOW COLOR LANGUAGE EVOLVED

yellow is absorbing knowledge

Yellow is the lightest color in the spectrum. It is a search for a more realistic perspective that will create hope and a brighter tomorrow. Likewise, people who prefer yellow have the ability to study situations and relationships without a preconceived mindset. Yellows are concerned with understanding the world around them.

blue is being cohesive

Blue is the coldest color in our atmosphere. Likewise, people who prefer blue are able to deny the natural warmth and energy of the present to anticipate the future. Like water, which bonds together, those who prefer blue pull together different entities to form a cohesive focus. Blue is future-based thought. It's about initiating dreams.

red is directing

Red directs physical change. Whether it is the molten lava inside the center of the earth, a fire burning in a forest, or an indicator of bacteria on an organism, red is the agent of change on earth. Likewise, people who prefer red are constantly improving on the status quo. Red is about directing resources.

WHEN YOUR PRIMARY COLORS CHANGE

Generally speaking, your favorite primary color does not change after your early twenties. If you are questioning your life goals, it can change until you become more comfortable with yourself. Your least favorite primary color is the last to change. If it changes, you're probably in a highly reactive period of your life.

THE PRIMARY IQ
ANSWER TRUE OR FALSE

yellow favorite primary color
1. Is threatening in the workplace. T or F
2. Is flexible. T or F

yellow least favorite primary color
3. Rarely has to do things twice. T or F
4. Can be a real jerk. T or F

blue favorite primary color
5. Lives for their dreams. T or F
6. Is realistic about ideas. T or F

blue least favorite primary color
7. Is hungry for marriage. T or F
8. Talks to him/herself a lot. T or F

red favorite primary color
9. Says what they think. T or F
10. Never discusses other people. T or F

red least favorite primary color
11. Blurts out how they feel. T or F
12. Knows more about everyone. T or F

* Answers on the next page

ANSWERS TO THE PRIMARY QUIZ

yellow favorite primary color
1.   F   They are about as threatening as a puppy dog.
2.   T   They are so flexible, they can become your fantasy of the moment.

yellow least favorite primary color
3.   F   Their faster-than-a-speeding-bullet personality can really blow it the first time.
4.   T   If they know what they want, you better get out of their way.

blue favorite primary color
5.   T   Just ask about them, and get ready for an earful.
6.   F   Is there ice water in hell?

blue least favorite primary color
7.   F   The idea of walking down the aisle makes them shake.
8.   T   They're their own best friend.

red favorite primary color
9.   T   Like Madonna, Oprah, or Mae West.
10.   F   Only if their jaws are wired shut!

red least favorite primary color
11.   F   Not unless they're pushed, tipsy, or ticked off.
12.   T   Ask them, they probably know lots about you.

HOW YOU RELATE

Green, purple, and orange make up the secondary category. They determine how you reason in your relationships and create bonds with the world around you. The harmonic vibrations of the secondary colors can be soothing or irritating. Green is the child of yellow and blue; purple is the child of blue and red; orange is the child of red and yellow. Before you begin, make your secondary color selections from page 22.

IN THIS CHAPTER

YOU WILL LEARN MORE about how other people affect your priorities, needs, choices, failures, job performance, and contributions.

YOUR FAVORITE SECONDARY COLOR reveals your actual thinking process when it comes to your desires, needs, and goals. It shows how you relate to others.

YOUR LEAST FAVORITE SECONDARY COLOR represents your subliminal needs that are often ignored. It is your emotional way of confronting what you want from other people.

SECONDARY COLORS REFLECT

The secondary colors translate the world around you into language. They reflect your thinking process. What do you consider first? Last? As you read this chapter, consider the pluses and minuses of the way you prioritize facts and feelings. Simple awareness of your thinking will make you a star.

SECONDARY NOTES

green

"The purest and
most thoughtful minds
are those that love
color the most."

JOHN RUSKIN

your thoughts

You're the perfect audience for others' problems. They interpret your concerns as encouragement to talk about their lives. They feel you can see beyond outward appearances and truly understand who they are. Like fertile soil, you nurture people so that their dreams can grow.

You are initially open to the world. In fact, you probably liked most of the colors in The Dewey Color System™! You appear innocent, but your curiosity makes you quite knowledgeable. You know about life, either through your own activities or through listening to others.

what turns you on and off

You understand people's true intentions. When talking with someone you've just met, or with friends and lovers, at first you put their needs before your own. This allows you to walk in their shoes and see how they feel inside. Then, you step back to objectively view their intentions. You see others for who they really are.

key words
NURTURING
CONCERNED
COMFORTABLE

power
CREATING
SUPPORTIVE
ENVIRONMENTS

motivation
TO UNDERSTAND WHO
YOU ARE AND WHAT
YOU WANT

green

You are attracted to someone who is intellectually inspiring. Intelligence is a real turn-on. It entices your curiosity. Even when there's absolutely no physical attraction, you are still able to maintain a friendship. Sometimes this can be confusing to the other person, because your initial attraction can be misinterpreted.

You marry or commit for security. This might mean having a home with children, having lots of money, being cared about, or just having a stabilizing personality in your life. Sometimes the physical or mental characteristics of the person you marry are sufficient to give you this sense of security. Whatever form it takes, the need for security is the key factor in your decision making.

your natural talents

You are practical and reliable. Everyone appreciates how supportive you are and how you establish a nurturing environment. You're a natural at managing their talents. In fact, you are excellent at managing materials and financial resources.

These qualities allow you to deal with the public. They support your ability to do well in professions that include interviewing, training, counseling, or working with children. You need to work for a company that will be consistent in its employment policies. This will allow you to feel secure about your future.

As you mature, seeking a stable career position will increase in importance. If your practical affairs aren't in order, you cannot be at peace. You need to be disciplined and work hard if you are to acquire material possessions. Some careers that will enhance your passions are banking, investing, insurance, business management, medicine, or consulting.

your life's a party when

...you know how others feel, and if they support and care about you. When people need you, you are there for them. You are good at listening to a person's problems and giving solid advice. Your concern for their well-being makes them feel more secure.

your hang ups occur when

...you question your identity. You can feel as if you are too close to someone and blame him or her for this dependence. You begin to withdraw and become consumed with yourself instead of being the supportive person that you normally are. This can shock or upset those who count on you. The more confident you are, the less this occurs.

be a star

Accept your sensitivity as a great gift, not a weakness. It will give you the strength to better support yourself and those around you. Cherish it and you will grow.

green

YOU SEEK TO BE NURTURED

You seek to be nurtured by providing for others. You need to believe that your concern for them will make them loyal to you. You will even sacrifice your own happiness. When you feel good, you remember to take care of yourself. When you are down, you have a tendency to avoid your supportive personal routine completely.

Your independent nature allows you to work for long periods of time without asking for help. You feel like an explorer. You go to extremes to make sure that co-workers and customers are happy. You are concerned for them, as if they were your children. You can in fact become so busy saving others that you lose yourself. Don't try to fix things until you've heard everything.

When you're upset, you become frustrated and emotionally spent. Only when you hit rock bottom do you realize what you need and tell others exactly what you want. It is as if you expect people to intuitively understand your needs. Like a child, you are hoping someone will care enough to notice. When you were growing up, did you believe you had to take on the responsibilities of an adult? Did you have to give support to your brothers or sisters or be there for one of your parents? Now, when you ask for help do you feel it signifies that you are weak and powerless?

Ask yourself every morning when you first get up, "What do I really need today, and who will support me after I tell them what I want?" Then listen to your feelings. Don't deny what you really want because of your concern for others. Selfishness for you would be a virtue. Everyone around you will be happier when you tell them what you want. The quicker you proclaim it, the better your relationships and life will become.

> ## "To think is to differ."
> CLARENCE DARROW

purple

your thoughts

Your search for personal power is certainly no secret. You are reflective and thoughtful. Others see you as witty, clever, and full of pride, and they are right. You need to show off your stuff. You are strong-willed. You know exactly what you want from others.

To say you can't achieve something is to say that you do not have possibilities in life. Others turn you on when they challenge you. It makes you work even harder. Your sense of drama wins people over. You are a great motivator. Your enthusiasm creates endless possibilities. You see significance in things that others miss. When your goal is defined, you are a leader and people are willing to follow you.

what turns you on and off

You are attracted to a person's energy. You don't really know why, you just are. Your decision to get married, though, is based on physical appearances, a special look that catches your eye. You can feel, for example, that someone was just "too cute" to let go. Attraction is difficult for you to deny when that special look is evident.

key words
DETERMINED
DRAMATIC
EMPOWERING

power
SEEING NEW
POSSIBILITIES, IDEAS,
AND STRATEGIES

motivation
TO BECOME MORE
SELF-POWERED

purple

Relationships mean serious business to you. You're loyal, but wary about forming new bonds. This can sometimes work to your detriment. Instead of experiencing life, you stand back, resisting what you know is right, analyzing yourself as if you were writing a book. You place your needs on a shelf to be dealt with later. Later, however, never comes.

Withdrawing emotionally is how you protect yourself. If you don't play the game, of course, you can't get hurt. All of a sudden you may realize that your friend or lover has become emotionally distant from you or is even gone. In denying yourself what you really needed, you have made them feel unimportant, as if you did not need them.

your natural talents

Everyone knows how easily you can come up with new ideas and ways of doing things. You salivate for a mental challenge. This makes you a natural in the business world. To construct something new is a big turn-on. It allows you to see your own potential. You love to be included in the developmental part of a project. In fact, you're going to tell them your idea, even if they don't ask.

Your dramatic expression helps motivate those around you. You encourage the potential in others. Your sharp tongue, however, can get you into lots of trouble, and sometimes people will not hear your message correctly. If your facts are exaggerated, others will lose faith in your information.

your life's a party when

...you look into the cause of things and analyze all the possibilities. You're the first to speak up, even when no one else will, and to take a stand against the crowd. Determined? You bet you are! No one stands in your way. You have the ability to do what those around you say you cannot do.

your hang ups occur when

...you assume things that have nothing to do with the other person's actual behavior. Dwelling on what should be or what could have been can lead to a lot of disappointment. You can become stuck analyzing your past experiences. Why someone did something is not for you to say. It can even make you loyal to a person who has not earned the privilege.

Your assumptions can make prioritizing what you want to do difficult. Be suspicious of yourself when you claim to be too charitable or feel emotionally wounded. You will make life a lot easier for everyone when you declare, not justify, your wants. Be especially careful of assuming you have changed. Small efforts are not enough. You must deal with the issues that real change requires.

be a star

Wisdom is gained by experiencing life. Constantly assuming what will happen only eliminates possibilities and diminishes your passion. Let each situation unfold on its own.

purple

YOU ARE LOGICAL

Facts come before feelings. You disregard emotions in order to get a more precise view of the people and situations around you. You clearly see when a relationship is not working and can end it without a lot of wasted energy. You have the talent of knowing what not to believe in. You choose your friends and lovers in a very objective way. You have lifetime friendships. It is almost as if to lose a friend is to lose memories.

In the workplace you are known for being very methodical. This gives you the ability to handle an emotionally charged situation and stay focused. You weigh only the pertinent facts and then set priorities.

When you're upset you stop communicating. You experience a mental burnout. Suddenly you become confronted with all of your hidden fears. Your deeply buried past feelings may not even be related to current issues. Yet, they still remain and can stop you from knowing how you feel in the present. During these crisis moments, your belief in people dwindles. You don't invest in the future or encourage others to believe in themselves.

Sometimes you make it uncomfortable for your loved ones to express themselves to you. This can lead to pent-up resentment, causing them to explode. Since you don't confront yourself with who you aren't, those around you don't either. This creates an information gap. Situations will arise where one moment everything is fine, and the next moment it's a disaster.

You forget things easily because your memory tends to be selective. You do not let your emotions interfere with your reasoning. You have a tendency to forget your dreams. To remember them might make your fear of knowing what is inside you a reality.

Your personal potential will only be realized when you allow yourself to be more forgiving of your emotions. Allow them to exist by trying not to rationalize everything.

> "A man is judged by
> what he does, not by
> what he says."
>
> ARISTOTLE

orange

your thoughts

You are dedicated to your job, hobbies, friends, and family. Your realistic view of the world allows you to identify what is not important. You are a doer and understand that eggs need to be broken if you want an omelet. You have a sharp eye for spotting physical things that are not working. Since you have the forcefulness of red, tempered with the awareness of yellow, you can get things done without ruffling feathers.

You're very sentimental. The older you become, the more you will have a tendency to talk about the past. If you have children and grandchildren, they'll get lots of affection from you. You're the first to show photos. You receive pleasure from placing photos of those you love all around the house.

You like physical activities. Driving fast cars, playing sports, and repairing things are some of the pastimes you might enjoy. You take pride in what you own and maintain your possessions. You have a bold approach to life.

key words
BOLD
SENTIMENTAL
DEDICATED

power
IMPLEMENTING
CHANGE WITHOUT
DISRUPTION

motivation
TO DISCOVER
HOW THINGS ARE
MADE

what turns you on and off

Everyone likes you. You're charismatic, lovable, affectionate, and big on hugs. After all, orange is the warmest color in our atmosphere. You are usually a hit at parties. You have a lot of friends. You need to touch others to know what they are made of. Touching gives you the ability to see the truth in situations and relationships. It is your way of letting others know you are listening and care about them. You build relationships with people who can teach you things.

When first meeting someone you hide the sensitive side of yourself. You are simply afraid to show the vulnerable you. Your defenses are all they see. They can even believe that you are somewhat formal or traditional.

You are lured into a relationship by the way a person looks. Your decision to get married, however, is based on intellect. You dedicate yourself to someone who is smart, and usually marry for life.

your natural talents

You're a very loyal employee who believes in what you do and whom you work for. You're the person who tells everyone how great your company is. When your employer does not return your appreciation by believing in and supporting you, your loyalty is quickly withdrawn. You have the ability to eliminate what is not important to you without expending much energy.

You unemotionally communicate the task at hand. Your co-workers respect you for being logical. Even when they disagree with you, they never see you as attacking them or their positions. After all, you're the one who usually has a clear, practical purpose in mind before starting a new project. You work best when there is constant social interaction. It especially turns you on to be needed. Chaos is no problem; you enjoy searching for solutions and doing a difficult task well.

your life's a party when

...you are dedicated. By boldly asking questions that others avoid, you figure out how things are made or how situations occurred. This allows you to make changes without disrupting or upsetting the status quo. By acting logically, not emotionally, you help others realize the truth. This is your talent. You make change less painful.

your hang ups occur when

...someone is critical of something you have done or should have done. You get defensive. It becomes a personal matter to you, one in which you feel that your dedication is being questioned. Your objectivity goes out the window. Don't make such a fuss. No one is questioning how much you care or how much you do. You care a lot and do more than your share.

be a star

Protect yourself by being dedicated to someone who is also dedicated to you. Loyalty for the right person or situation makes you feel secure and become successful.

YOU ARE OPEN TO THE WORLD

When you feel good, your naive approach to life can charm even the most jaded. Others see you as a considerate, nice person. When you feel bad, you distrust yourself or blame others. Your world becomes a bitter, lonely place.

When you first meet someone, you are either too serious or not serious enough. There is no middle ground. This may keep you from finding the relationships that you need. Being too serious hides the fun part of you, and being too carefree can make others think that you are not sincere.

At work, you're a natural at keeping customers and co-workers happy. You're concerned, considerate, and hard-working. Pleasing others motivates you. On the downside, your strong desire to please can make you commit to unrealistic deadlines. You can miss the practical realities of how long it takes to accomplish a task. You're then forced to overextend yourself, working so hard you become physically exhausted, even sick. Sure, sometimes you can accomplish a great deal of work, but is it really worth it?

Stop indulging your unrealistic expectations. Before you expect something from others or commit to doing something, ask more questions. You will see the underlying desires of others. Accept the fact that everyone is doing exactly what he or she wants to do, anyway. Aren't you doing what you really need to do, as well?

Evaluate your feelings. Make it your goal to eliminate what you do not want to do and who you do not enjoy being with. Only then will you realize what and who you need.

FINDING YOUR NICHE

THE COMBINATION OF YOUR FAVORITE AND LEAST FAVORITE SECONDARY COLOR SELECTIONS SHOWS HOW YOU RELATE TO OTHERS.

green favorite, purple least favorite

You listen for information, not feeling. Your flawless logic gives you the ability to calm those around you. You give them the power to prioritize the facts, not the feelings. Your dilemma in life is to be more comfortable with your emotions. You discount them before you have a chance to feel them. When you concentrate solely on the literal and factual, you destroy the human experiences you need to learn more about yourself.

green favorite, orange least favorite

Since people can read you like an open book, you often listen to their counsel. You can bond one-on-one with another person right away. Your dilemma in life is to learn how to share yourself without losing yourself. One moment you're concerned about your own needs, the next moment you're obsessing about other people. When you have the courage to disassociate from what you expect from yourself to see the truth of a situation, you'll know better who you are.

purple favorite, green least favorite

You encourage people to be the best that they can be. Being concerned for them inspires you and gives you new insights into your own power. If you feel you are rehearsing your expressions before you say them, beware. You're requesting something that's more about what you need than what the other person wants to give. Are you expecting to gain more control of a person if you are very nice to them? Don't be so responsible. Accept that your surroundings and how others feel are not about you, and you will learn how powerful you are.

purple favorite, orange least favorite

You listen to how powerful others can be to better understand your own desires. When you become concerned, you experience their passion. This allows you to better define what you enjoy. Your enthusiasm becomes unleashed passion. It starts new projects. You need to listen, however, for what you expect from others before you set out looking for exciting opportunities. Otherwise, you will become frustrated. Your overly high expectations of people and events can make you mistrustful when things don't turn out right. Then you start to whine about how you've been let down in the past.

orange favorite, purple least favorite

You have great concern for others, but sometimes you hide your feelings about people from yourself. You have strong analytical skills and know what is or is not important. At work, this is a helpful quality; at home, it can be a disaster. Your dilemma in life is to make sure that your deeply hidden emotions aren't negated by your logic. Give yourself the opportunity to feel the great love you have inside. Otherwise, you can become bitter and destroy the very core of who you are.

orange favorite, green least favorite

Your dedication to your work and those you love is boundless. There is nothing you will not do to make things work better. When you feel that those around you are not supporting you, however, you become very defensive. This defensiveness appears suddenly, because you hide your feelings—even from yourself. Try not to be overly dedicated. It is unhealthy for everyone involved if you completely lose yourself in causes and other people's problems.

GETTING IN SYNC

IF YOUR PARTNER, FRIEND, OR CO-WORKER SELECTED...

THE SAME FAVORITE SECONDARY COLOR AS YOU, they help you to understand the way you think more clearly.

A DIFFERENT FAVORITE SECONDARY COLOR THAN YOU, they show you a different way of viewing a situation or person.

a green with a green

Together, you create the feeling of being at home. At your best, you give each other a stronger sense of self. You feel as though you are one. To help the other is to help yourself. Both of you create a world that allows the other to better understand who they are. This is a secure place to be, a safe haven. At your worst, you see the other's selfish thoughts.

a purple with a purple

You assume many things. At your best, you both can create new ideas and develop new things. Your wit and sense of drama make life fun and exciting. Others can even believe the two of you are having an argument with your provoking sharp tongues and biting sarcasm, when in fact it's your way of having fun. You assume "facts" that are not correct. This can make you become both pessimistic and paranoid.

an orange with an orange

You reinforce each other's accomplishments. At your best, you create a world where you both feel appreciated. You constantly acknowledge how much the other has contributed to a project. Others see you as sentimental one moment and strictly logical the next. At your worst, you both can become overly critical and constantly examine unimportant things and minor transgressions.

a green with a purple

You increase each other's self-awareness and resiliency to transcend failure. As a green, you show a purple how to slow down and enjoy the pleasures of everyday life. In a crisis, you can become self-absorbed and ignore a purple's passion for the relationship.

As a purple, you help a green see empowering possibilities within him or her and become more self-confident. As a defense, you become entrenched in what you are doing, and ignore the green.

a green with an orange

You make people and things come together. As a green, you reinvigorate an orange by helping him or her stop focusing on past failures. The orange then stops being overly sensitive, and is better able to contribute to the world.

As an orange, your recognition of past accomplishments helps a green feel proud. But under stress, your compulsive dedication to others can make a green feel forgotten. You then turn critical, annoyed by the green's need for "constant" attention.

a purple with an orange

You create realistic dreams. As a purple, you teach an orange to see the possibilities of the future. In turn, the orange's analytical side makes your expectations more realistic.

As an orange, you become negative when the purple is distracted by grandiose ideas. If you appear too consumed by others or your job, the purple can feel left out and unimportant.

YOUR SECONDARY CONNECTION

IF YOU LIKE TWO SECONDARY CATEGORY COLORS EQUALLY, you are uncertain about what you want out of a relationship. Others can feel that they know you, and then an entirely different person appears. Confusing? You bet you are! No one can please you or even be close to you unless they know what you need.

IF YOU PREFERRED THE COLORS IN THE SECONDARY CATEGORY OVERALL, you are always thinking about others. You can be excessive in your need to be close to someone. This is especially evident in a crisis. You completely lose yourself. Always thinking about others makes it difficult for them to give back to you.

IF YOU FIND THE SECONDARY CATEGORY COLORS DISTURBING, you are bitter from a past relationship or not available emotionally. To you, these colors are too open to the world. Stop identifying with those sad love songs on the radio! Show your vulnerability by letting your significant other or a possible relationship candidate think for you.

laughing out loud

When I owned a staffing company, I trained hundreds of sales representatives. Most of them preferred purple—just like me. Driving back from sales calls, we purples would always assume we knew what the client needed, instead of asking them. It was really scary. Agreement somehow made our logical deductions facts. Later we would be shocked that our information was erroneous.

The sales representatives who preferred green had a natural consultant approach. They used their listening skills to build client rapport. Their nurturing, yet conclusive approach made each client feel more in charge. Those who preferred purple were amazed that such a low-key approach could make a sale.

I had many oranges that were successful in sales. When they were dedicated, they would go to war, not to work. Hands-on projects allowed them to get really involved with fixing everything. They preferred working with more tangible items or projects.

HOW COLOR LANGUAGE EVOLVED

green is nurturing

Green provides the nurturing infrastructure for life. Fertile soil contains the ingredients that allow plants to grow. Likewise, people who prefer green are nurturing and are aware of the delicate balance that our environment demands. They understand the most basic needs and provide the infrastructure for physical existence.

purple is seeing possibilities

Purple is the darkest color in the spectrum. Likewise, people who prefer purple are looking to define themselves. They have the courage to look into the darkness of their emotions. A purple is concerned with defining the self to become more powerful. They know that personal growth starts with considering the possibilities.

orange is dissecting

Orange is the warmest color in our atmosphere. Heat is the force of change. It separates matter. Likewise, the separation of each element gives a person who prefers orange the ability to analyze how things were made. Then, like osmosis, they eliminate what is and isn't working so the new can grow. An orange is concerned with creating constructive change.

WHEN YOUR SECONDARY COLORS CHANGE

The degree to which you like your favorite secondary color determines how involved you are in your personal and professional relationships. If it changes, you are going through a tough relationship period. If your least favorite secondary color changes abruptly, you have learned a great lesson about those around you.

THE SECONDARY IQ
ANSWER TRUE OR FALSE

green favorite secondary color
1. Is innocent in both thoughts and actions.   T or F
2. Is turned on by intelligence.   T or F

green least favorite secondary color
3. Loves to be nurtured by others.   T or F
4. Needs to be more selfish.   T or F

purple favorite secondary color
5. Doesn't like talking about ideas or developing new things.   T or F
6. When insulted, initially gets quiet.   T or F

purple least favorite secondary color
7. Shows their emotions to everyone.   T or F
8. When upset, says nothing.   T or F

orange favorite secondary color
9. When bored, creates chaos.   T or F
10. Can be sentimental, even sappy.   T or F

orange least favorite secondary color
11. Can be too nice.   T or F
12. Is good at eliminating what's not working.   T or F

★   Answers on the next page

ANSWERS TO THE SECONDARY QUIZ

green favorite secondary color
1. F   Don't let that sweet face fool you.
2. T   They are having an intimate moment with your mind.

green least favorite secondary color
3. T   Cooking them a meal is a big deal.
4. T   They could take selfish lessons.

purple favorite secondary color
5. F   They will give you their opinions even if you don't ask.
6. T   Then, they get even.

purple least favorite secondary color
7. F   Even their lovers don't know them.
8. T   In a personal crisis, "good morning" is an effort.

orange favorite secondary color
9. T   Watch out. Somehow they will get you to stir up the day.
10. T   Pictures and stories can be nonstop.

orange least favorite secondary color
11. T   Listen to them. "Can I help you?"
12. F   They continue doing things the wrong way until they pass out.

WHO YOU ARE

Your favorite primary color, your motivation, together with your favorite secondary color, how you relate, reveals your self-concept.

Knowing who you really are and what you want will better equip you to handle and solve life's problems. It will give you a better understanding of how to have more passion in your life, relationships, and career. Before you begin, select your favorite primary and secondary colors from page 22.

IN THIS CHAPTER

YOU WILL VIEW HOW YOU SEE YOURSELF. Self-knowledge is empowering. From it comes the confidence to do what you do best.

PAY ATTENTION TO YOUR THOUGHTS. What passionate part of yourself are you able to express? Not express?

CELEBRATE YOURSELF

Here's your chance to be affirmed for your greatness. Stress, constantly striving to make money, or being consumed by what needs to be done can distract you from celebrating yourself. Personal growth begins with accepting yourself just as you are right now. As you read this chapter, celebrate the unique talents and power within you by reviewing the contributions and gifts you have given to others.

COLOR NOTES

THE CARETAKERS

Your realistic perspective creates comfortable and secure environments for yourself and those around you. You listen to what others say and see their point of view. By questioning what people really need instead of accepting what they think they need, you help them learn.

Taking care of other people is your purpose and natural talent. However, when you're overprotective, you're not doing anyone any favors. Don't interfere with others' ability to discover their own needs. Constantly rescuing people denies them the opportunity to confront their own responsibilities. So step back and allow them to be themselves without your support. If they should fail, that's okay. Only then will they be able to distinguish what they ought to be doing.

Since you sympathize with the perspective of the people in your life, it can be difficult for you to be objective about yourself. Try to forget about your surroundings and focus on your own needs. This will enable others to give you better support and keep you from neglecting your own happiness.

IF YOU LIKE YELLOW MORE THAN GREEN, you are more realistic about your own personal growth and career advancement than you are about your relationships.

IF YOU LIKE GREEN MORE THAN YELLOW, you tend to be more realistic about your relationships and less directive about achieving your goals.

yellow and green

COLOR NOTES

THE CATALYSTS

yellow and purple

You are on a journey to discover your passion for life. Change fuels your inner fire. First you experience your environment, and then you stand back and analyze it. This sparks your growth and your concerns. You see the value of each moment and have fun when you're committed to personal growth.

Your knowledge of spiritual truths inspires others to discover their own spirituality. Your curious, investigative nature enhances your intuitive powers. You help others become self-aware. By actively listening, making clever observations, and expressing your feelings, you spark the passions of others to initiate positive change.

You are a great communicator. You have the ability to listen without bias, and understand the possibilities of what could be. During conversations, you are a powerhouse. You see right through things and grasp the real essence of what needs to be done. You are at your best, personally and professionally, when you are communicating.

In your obsession with change, you become too concerned about the issues and items of your world. Use your natural talent to know what is real, yet see the possibilities. Simply believe in yourself and you will make the right move. You know how to make positive changes.

IF YOU LIKE YELLOW MORE THAN PURPLE, you first consider the reality of a situation, then you see the possibilities.

IF YOU LIKE PURPLE MORE THAN YELLOW, you consider the possibilities for other people and things before you consider your own future.

COLOR NOTES

THE TECHNICAL THINKERS

Your first thoughts are about how to get things done. By establishing a systematic approach, you better understand tasks, relationships, even life. Your realism makes others see you as technical. You see yourself as one who maximizes resources.

You playfully examine the talents and resources around you. Your experimental approach allows the world to reveal itself to you. This discovery gives you the power to put these talents and resources to better use.

Fun means being emotionally committed to investigating how all the facts fit together. You examine successful parts of a task or relationship as if you were putting together a puzzle. Each piece is a resource or a personal value that can be used to make something new, or to reinvent a relationship. To the amazement of others, you create something original from what already exists.

Under pressure, your technical approach helps you to see what has not been done. This can make others defensive. They see you as being formal or rigid. Since you are usually the first to notice when someone has made a mistake, you make people worry.

Be especially careful if you are in an unstimulating environment. Without new information steadily coming in, you can find yourself in a rut. Others will view you as negative or nitpicking. In actuality, you feel lost and are searching to find what you want.

IF YOU LIKE YELLOW MORE THAN ORANGE, your own personal growth comes before your relationships.

IF YOU LIKE ORANGE MORE THAN YELLOW, you think of what others need before you think of yourself.

yellow and orange

COLOR NOTES

THE ANCHORS

You have fun nurturing and supporting others. Your endless curiosity entices them to tell you what they are thinking. You see people's dreams and are sensitive to their needs. You give them the self-confidence to believe in their own capabilities. Your concerns make them feel important. Your listening grounds them.

At first, you have a need to fit in. Others can assume you are like them. Then the real you appears. Now they must reacquaint themselves with a person they thought they already knew. This new you might have less in common with them than they believed. Because of this disparity, you sometimes attract situations and relationships that don't provide you with what you need.

You listen intensely. You want to know how others feel. This gives you the ability to hear music and languages better. If the opportunity is available, you can play an instrument well and pronounce your language or other languages with less of an accent. You are articulate.

When you become too comfortable or too earnest, you neglect your personal growth and relationships. Be more conclusive about what you expect. Only then will others know how to contribute and your life will be more pleasing.

IF YOU LIKE BLUE MORE THAN GREEN, your career or personal goals are your first priority. Your relationships need to agree with your dreams.

IF YOU LIKE GREEN MORE THAN BLUE, you're supportive of others' dreams before your own.

blue and green

COLOR NOTES

THE THINKERS

You ponder existence. You need to know why things are. The conclusions you come to allow you to see the big picture. Your understanding of why things are needed enables you to make improvements. By focusing on the future, you think of ideas and things as if they were already completed. You live in this future vision. It's a picture in your head.

You are at your best when you understand human motivation and the laws of cause and effect. You are constantly categorizing things to create plans of action. Without these plans, it can be difficult for you to be organized. You become a scattered daydreamer.

You are a trailblazer. When you're committed to developing new ideas and structures you have fun. Making the ideas in your head a reality allows your passions to soar. When your faith is strong, you can assume things, regardless of the truth. False assumptions about yourself or others can throw you off base.

Your constant need to do something new can keep you from appreciating what you have done. Too many pictures in your head can make your life difficult. Situations or other people will not measure up. Unknowingly, you can ask for the unattainable, especially from yourself.

IF YOU LIKE BLUE MORE THAN PURPLE, you consider your dreams first and your relationships second.

IF YOU LIKE PURPLE MORE THAN BLUE, you are more concerned about how to be more powerful with your existing relationships.

blue and purple

COLOR NOTES

THE BUILDERS

You demand an exciting life. You create it with your dual personality. One moment you are the innovative freethinker who wishes to construct a new modular home and the next moment you shift gears and become a traditional critic, questioning why anyone would undertake such a thing. You are a social enigma.

Your curiosity sparks chaotic conversations. You thrive on them. This makes you fun at parties. Your friends are a bunch of characters with very diverse interests. Sometimes you stop and wonder how you keep finding yourself amidst such craziness. But deep down you know that too much order in a social environment can restrict people's growth.

You want to believe that the world needs you. Often, you become preoccupied with trying to make sense of social situations over which you have no control. In the end, you feel frustrated and emotionally depleted. You must realize that the world is never going to be a perfect place. You can only do so much, and will be most effective if you focus on improving your immediate surroundings.

If you're not dedicated to a cause, it's impossible for you to be constructive. When you are in a situation where you cannot give your all, move on. You need to be building something or you will get depressed.

IF YOU LIKE BLUE MORE THAN ORANGE, you consider how to build something new first, then critique your plan.

IF YOU LIKE ORANGE MORE THAN BLUE, it's easy for you to get caught up in the thrill of the moment and forget your plans.

blue and orange

COLOR NOTES

THE RESOURCE MANAGERS

Practical and nurturing, you teach others how to achieve more value in their lives. No one fools you. You're a dynamic personality and know exactly what everyone is up to. You've got a knack for knowing what is important. Like a parent or a teacher, you are concerned about how to make people's lives better. Helping others gives you self-respect.

You are at your best when you are directing the use of resources. You start out very nurturing but become very authoritative and even bossy. There is no middle ground. You are either one or the other. This can be confusing to those around you. People don't always realize that even when you're bossy you're looking out for their best interests.

When you are upset, under pressure, or intoxicated, you favor your expressive red side. Without the calming effects of green, you can really shock your friends with outrageous behavior. If you like green more than red, this characteristic is even more dramatic. If others act differently toward you during this period, it is because they don't feel they know you.

IF YOU LIKE RED MORE THAN GREEN, you consider what things are needed before you think of others. This allows you to be direct and confident.

IF YOU LIKE GREEN MORE THAN RED, your supportive nature wins out and you initially direct your energy toward what other people need.

red and green

COLOR NOTES

THE SYNTHESIZERS

You enjoy integrating the factual and emotional aspects of situations. After something has occurred, you analyze the event, cut out the nonsense, and pull people together to make things work better. Others see your need for order as somewhat formal. You are at your best when you allow yourself to give advice or be direct. Being supportive makes you feel complete.

Your body language attracts people. Your curiosity generates action. You are sexy. New things may excite and regenerate you, but they can also distract you from finishing what you need to do. Don't procrastinate; finish things before your passion dwindles.

You need to know that situations and people are who they claim to be. This is especially evident when you're in a bad mood. You become very controlling of your environment. You see only what isn't. People find you so skeptical and overanalytical that everyone's mood is spoiled. You need the capability to synthesize feelings and situations into a workable plan. Otherwise, directing your future will feel like a hardship.

IF YOU LIKE RED MORE THAN PURPLE, you're more interested in making things work than you are in winning popularity contests. You can tend, though, to speak before you consider the consequences.

IF YOU LIKE PURPLE MORE THAN RED, you're more concerned about people's reactions. You use your charm and guile to get what you want done.

COLOR NOTES

THE HUMANITARIANS

You honor individuality. You believe in walking your own path and speaking your own mind without apologies. If someone gets out of line, you're not about to keep quiet. You're looking for unconditional love, and hope to create an environment where everyone can express himself or herself without fear of embarrassment.

You prefer the intimate company of the people you're close to. Big is not necessarily better for you. Small towns, small companies, and small groups of friends hold greater rewards. They allow you to feel important. Otherwise, excessive concerns, situations, friends, or even emotions can eliminate your ability to see the truth.

You perceive what is not working for others. Then, ready or not, you tell them about it. This can frighten away those who are not secure with themselves. Others see you as loyal and protective.

Your action-oriented personality hides your sensitive side. This is a defense mechanism. Open up. Show some vulnerability. You will, like a magnet, attract the love and respect that you deserve.

IF YOU LIKE RED MORE THAN ORANGE, you're more preoccupied with your ability to make positive changes than you are with your relationships.

IF YOU LIKE ORANGE MORE THAN RED, you're more apt to be a facilitator and fix things for the common good.

IDENTIFY YOUR ROLE MODEL

Your color preference is inherited. Check out your parents and children. Evaluations have indicated that even three-generation color matches are common. Read your family birth order below.

OLDEST BOY OR GIRL IN A FAMILY, you probably prefer the same colors as your parents or grandparents. For example, if one of your parents is a blue-purple, and the other is a yellow-green, you will select their same colors or the colors of your grandparents.

MIDDLE CHILD, you share both of your parents' colors. If you had problems coping, chances are your favorite choices are one of your parent's least favorite choices, not favorite.

YOUNGEST, AN ONLY CHILD, OR SEPARATED FROM YOUR OTHER SIBLING BY AT LEAST SEVEN YEARS, chances are even stronger that you have adopted the colors of one of your parents.

your mainframe

In this chapter, you have read about your favorite primary and secondary category colors. The primaries—yellow, blue, and red—allow you to express your main energy in life. The secondaries—green, purple, and orange—allow you to bond with those around you. Together, they create your mainframe.

8 chapter

YOUR HOPES AND FEARS

Black, brown, and white fall into the achromatic category because they are not in the chromatic spectrum. They represent your inner self. This instinctual part of you is the glue that holds you together. It is the underlying force behind all your hopes and fears. Before you begin, select your achromatic colors from page 23.

IN THIS CHAPTER

YOU'LL LEARN HOW TO ALLOW THE SILENCE WITHIN YOU TO EXIST. Working too hard, thinking too much, or substance abuse will make it difficult for you to experience your inner feelings.

YOUR FAVORITE ACHROMATIC COLOR is the core of you rationally directing change. You are trying to make sure your inner self is getting what it needs most.

YOUR LEAST FAVORITE ACHROMATIC COLOR shows what deep-rooted concerns inhibit the pursuit of your passions. It is you making sure that your inner self is confronting your greatest dilemmas.

ACHROMATIC COLORS COMPLETE YOU

The achromatic colors display your reaction when pressure is forcing you to change. You will see what you treasure most about yourself, as well as your greatest flaw. As you read this chapter, be especially tuned in to the voice inside of you that is only apparent when you are completely silent.

ACHROMATIC NOTES

> "We function on feeling. When you know the magic, you will always find a place in the Kingdom."
>
> WALT DISNEY

your hopes

You know the value each person brings to a relationship. Others see you as an impetuous, forceful, self-protective person. You want to know about the unknown. You try to map your life into a logical plan about the future. At decision time, your feelings can override rationality.

Your commitment to others provides you with a healthy perspective of yourself. You passionately extend yourself to others. When you get too close and they reject you, your feelings play back an emotional review of your life. Contemplating past emotional feelings makes you feel secure and gives you the sense that you are on the right path.

your fears

You take people and events too seriously. This makes it hard, sometimes impossible, for you to remain objective. You tend to shift the blame on someone or something else if things don't go your way. Much of your misery is caused by not letting go of the past. Retreating into your memories only compounds your problems.

key words
EMOTIONAL
FOCUSED
LOYAL

power
TO KNOW
YOUR EMOTIONS

motivation
TO UNDERSTAND
YOUR PAST

When you become upset, you exaggerate your responsibilities and feel overwhelmed. Only when you're emotionally frustrated do you consider making changes. Starting a new course of action makes you feel guilty, as if you're betraying others or losing yourself.

feed your soul

You find it sexy when others need you. It allows you to feel close to them, even safe. Being close to others makes you feel that the world cannot hurt you. When others encourage you to express how you feel, it turns you on.

You feel very responsible for those around you. This makes those you care about feel comfortable. They know where you stand. It can also, however, make you too predictable. If you don't already, make it a point to blow it out occasionally. Keep it spicy!

unstuff your relationships

When you feel that others aren't giving you emotional support, you try to get even closer. Take a step back and give them the space they need. Don't let your need to be emotionally attached push them away. If you feel pain, it is all about your denial to accept something that is occurring. Don't be so needy. Your defensiveness will negatively affect your self-confidence and make it difficult to be close to you.

getting it done

You're disciplined and keep others in line. When you are loyal or have ownership, you fight to keep what is yours. You're an overachiever and need autonomy to be at your best. You like to get things finished without being interrupted. Still, you need for co-workers to be loyal to you and, in turn, you are genuinely concerned about them.

get your act together

Your need to complete everything can hamper your ability to be open to essential information. This stubborn streak will be your downfall. Don't let your determination make you miss the obvious. Listen for new options, even after your decision is made. Let others contribute. Many times, new ways of doing things will actually complement your way.

your great lesson

Your memories are the treasures of your spirit. They belong only to you. Honor them by not getting tangled up in your emotions. Learn from them and move forward.

black

YOU MAKE UNEMOTIONAL DECISIONS

black LEAST FAVORITE

You are very rational. At decision time, you are unemotional. This detachment helps you connect new ideas and information. Using only logic, you can see where others are excessive and inconsistent. You cut to the truth to focus on what needs to be done.

In your relationships, you become very attached and your emotions overwhelm you. Completely losing yourself can be a major turn-on. Later, however, you can experience an empty feeling, as if you have lost yourself. Ending a relationship at first appears to be easy for you, but releasing the emotions is difficult. You need to understand that still having feelings after the fact doesn't mean you should go back and change your decision.

In the workplace, you are driven and desire advancement. You expect others to recognize your level-headed way of doing business. You wish to make your own schedule without having to report to a superior. Under pressure, you become very logical. This is the exact opposite of what happens in your relationships. When the pressure is really tough, co-workers seek you out for an unbiased perspective. Helping them solve their problems makes you feel special.

Get in touch with your emotions. Try not to be so logical all the time. If you follow your heart instead of your head, you will be happier in the long run. You'll better understand the value of your commitments, and any changes occurring in your life will better fit your needs. You will gain the power to better direct those "illogical feelings."

> "The only man who can
> change his mind is
> the man who's
> got one."
>
> EDWARD NOYES WESTCOTT

your hopes

You give the gift of knowledge. Your suggestions make others slow down and consider all the options. Your objectivity gives you and others the ability to consider things thoroughly. When you get what you wish, your hope is renewed. You bring optimistic agendas and problem-solving skills to situations.

Your satisfaction is linked to navigating options successfully. You desire to better evaluate all things so you can connect them to your goals. The world is yours for the taking if you can distinguish subtle differences between options. By logically analyzing things before taking action, you have the power to plot the future you want.

key words
OBJECTIVE
CURIOUS
ANALYTICAL

power
TO SEE NEW OPTIONS

motivation
TO CREATE A
NEW FUTURE

your fears

Under pressure, you step back to gain objectivity. However, too much distance can cause you to lose sight of what's important to you. It can keep you from making the best of existing situations. Slow down. Remember to give your feelings equal power. You will better know what you want. Your world will feel more solid.

feed your soul

When you have enough space, everyone benefits. Distance in your situations and relationships gives you the power not to get bogged down with problems. You also gain the ability to tell people about new ways to make their lives work better.

unstuff your relationships

You have a tendency to avoid getting close to people. You immerse yourself in new schemes and overload yourself with information. Is it any wonder, then, that people can feel you are self-absorbed and not committed to them? Under stress they may even feel that you've severed the relationship without saying good-bye. Decide what makes you happy and cleanly cut things from your life that aren't working. Allow your future to be determined by the actions you take, not the results of your inaction.

getting it done

You are at your best when you can give advice on new and better ways of doing things. You adapt well to changing situations. Environments where you can meet new people and experience new things invigorate your natural curiosity. All this stimulation enhances your charm. It allows you to appreciate who and what is important to you.

get your act together

Don't let your search to find the perfect solution destroy your ability to make decisions. Be decisive. There are no guarantees in life. Failing to make timely decisions will only make matters worse. Constantly looking for new options can also make others feel unimportant. They can lose their loyalty to you or feel that you do not have confidence in them. Prioritize what is already working.

your great lesson

Clearly communicate your need for extra space in your relationships in order to see things objectively. Once others understand your nature, they will better appreciate your valuable suggestions.

white

YOU MAKE OTHERS BELONG

When your spirit soars, you attract others like a magnet. Talking to you makes them feel that they belong. This helps you fit in. When you feel bad, change is almost impossible. Many times you retreat right before you try to end something. Your fear of abandonment can stop you from starting over, even when situations are harmful to you.

When you start to make a change in your life you panic. You see too many options, which can make you feel confused or frustrated. This state is only temporary. Concentrate on distancing yourself. Don't worry, you won't lose what's important to you. In fact, you'll see more clearly what you value in life.

In comfortable work situations, your very presence makes things come together. Your energy inspires closer teamwork among co-workers. You run into trouble, however, when you do not consider all the options. Have you investigated and considered all your possible resources? Have you gotten input from the vendors, the department heads, your co-workers? Be careful. If you wait until the last minute, you might miss opportunities or make extra work for yourself.

When you don't have to be thinking about someone or something else, you will know the pleasure of being alive. You will be able to take risks, see new things, and meet exciting people. Try imagining yourself lying on a beach. Who do you want there with you? Why? Who did not get invited? Why not? Knowing where you stand will allow you to feel a lot more secure.

> "The world is a looking glass and gives back to every man the reflection of his own face."
>
> WILLIAM MAKEPEACE THACKERAY

brown

your hopes

You are down-to-earth. By recognizing your superficial aspects, you become authentic. For the most part you do not believe in an afterlife, divine judgment, or cruel fate. Things just exist. Everything else is vanity. You are able to weigh all the available options, thinking twice before making a decision. Others might see you as intuitive. But in reality you are simply free of illusions and well aware of the consequences of your actions.

You prefer to live in the moment and appreciate the pleasures of life. You are inspired by the charms of the world. The more you experience your environment, the more you express yourself. Doing is exciting. Activity makes you feel more complete. You are constantly looking for new sensations to spice up your life.

key words
AWARE
AUTHENTIC
COMPASSIONATE

power
TO UNDERSTAND
REALITY

motivation
TO EXPERIENCE THE
SENSATIONS OF LIFE

your fears

Your fears are based on physical realities. Death, decay, aging, and loss of faculties and happiness are your concerns. You worry that your dedication has caused you to neglect important areas of your own life. Then, when you declare what you want, others can see you as selfish. Step back before you act. Notice how each person contributes to your life. Do they respect your knowledge? Is your loyalty appreciated?

feed your soul

You wish to indulge your passions and live to the fullest. You often have an exaggerated look of concentration in your eyes. Your strong awareness of others' needs creates energy. It turns you on and allows you to get what or whom you want. This is your power. You don't take things personally and refrain from judgment. You realize that each person is out for himself or herself. That's just the way of life.

unstuff your relationships

When upset, you can become fixated on what you want, determined to get it no matter what the consequences are. Is your dedication to others or situations keeping you from experiencing your own desires? Before you grab for what you want, confront your feelings. Otherwise, your obsessive nature can cause people to feel neglected and to question their worth.

getting it done

As a manager, you fully comprehend situations before issuing commands. You prefer to work in an environment where you can be very supportive and keep others aware of the day-to-day realities. Your realistic thinking helps you make the most out of physical resources. You think about making things better now, not later, and don't dwell on the past. Others are comforted by your keen awareness.

get your act together

When you constantly ask questions to try to ascertain the facts, others can assume you are less knowledgeable than you really are. They don't understand you're trying to cut through everyone's subjective viewpoint. This is a big concern and could lead to your being passed over and denied the recognition you deserve. Make sure to let others know what you've accomplished.

your great lesson

Don't try to be everything to those you are committed to. Instead, focus on being deeply involved and committed to experiencing your life. You'll become more alive.

brown

NOTHING CAN STOP YOU

You're an alumnus of the school of hard knocks. By learning the hard way, you have experienced things you never would have if things had been easier. You are determined to make changes. You feel that you can change your environment and yourself and nothing can stop you.

As you get older, you notice things are different. Everyone has gotten older. Don't obsess about time creeping up on you. Accept that your viewpoint will change, you will look older, and some younger people will not find you as sexy. Enjoy yourself at each stage of your life.

You can sometimes feel that you are aggressively pushing yourself to get what you want and are going nowhere, or that you've spent too long waging everyone else's battles. Look again. Aren't you avoiding facts that you know all too well? At first, becoming more aware of what you're capable of and what you can expect from your relationships will feel like an ice-cold shower. Later, however, you will feel marvelous, more alive.

At work, you can ask too much of yourself or others. Take things as they come. Do not expect others to protect you. You'll feel more grounded and more in control. Be honest with yourself and accept limitations. Denying what capabilities a job or career requires will only frustrate you in the end. You won't be any wiser from the experience.

Ultimately, life is only as rich as your experiences. Regularly remind yourself that you are going to die. You will treasure more what you are doing and attract friends and relationships who will allow you to savor life more deeply.

PREDICTING OUTCOMES

THE COMBINATION OF YOUR FAVORITE AND LEAST FAVORITE ACHROMATIC COLOR SELECTION SHOWS HOW YOU CONFRONT CHANGE.

black favorite, white least favorite

You rely on your emotional awareness to improve your relationships. You are very dedicated and your loyalty to those around you makes you greatly loved. Unfortunately, when a change is needed, you have a tendency to dwell on things excessively. You can stay in a situation or relationship long after it has ended. Prioritize what is important and then go out and make your own luck.

black favorite, brown least favorite

Your emotions make you feel powerful. Regardless of the distractions in life, you see the value of things. Your loyalty to others helps them become better people, which is probably why you have such devoted people around you. However, when making decisions you sometimes have unrealistic expectations of others. So, be careful. Accept things as they are, not how they could be, and people will not let you down as much. Your life will be more satisfying. You will feel more like a winner.

white favorite, black least favorite

Logical and practical, you easily find new ways of achieving your goals. But because you keep your emotions tightly under wrap and maintain your distance, people can find you cold. Being of a critical nature doesn't help you either. You may find getting really close to someone in a relationship is difficult. To become emotionally attached seems irrational to you. You feel as if you are losing your objectivity.

white favorite, brown least favorite

You constantly assess yourself and others. However, the options that you see for yourself are often beyond your ability to accomplish or may not be what you really want. You spend too much energy on the search and not enough thought about where you really want to go. Distancing yourself from your feelings and other people doesn't help any. Are you afraid to confront your desires? Deal with them. Determine where they will lead you, or you will destroy your ability to hold on to what is most important to you.

brown favorite, black least favorite

You are very realistic. It is very difficult to fool you. You base your decisions on the facts. At the start others see you as concerned about them. All of a sudden, though, you seem only to care about what's right and not about people's feelings. You are an overachiever, but all this activity can get in the way of understanding yourself. Remember that you are more than just the sum of your achievements. Confront your emotions. Otherwise, you will only define yourself in respect to how others see you.

brown favorite, white least favorite

You are very realistic and have an innate sense of fairness. You use facts to pull things together. Others think of you as being very sensitive to them. Regrettably, all of this attention paid to others distracts you from thinking about yourself. Be more objective. Take a moment to decide what else you could have in life or your obsessive routines will destroy your future.

SEXUAL CHEMISTRY

IF YOUR PARTNER, FRIEND, OR CO-WORKER SELECTED...

THE SAME FAVORITE ACHROMATIC COLOR AS YOU, they allow you to better piece together your inner self. They make you feel good about yourself.

A DIFFERENT FAVORITE ACHROMATIC COLOR THAN YOU, they make you aware of your greatest lessons in life. They give you the knowledge to succeed.

a black with a black

...has a genuine appreciation of how loyal the other one is to those they care about. You make each other feel good about the decisions and sacrifices you have made in your lives on behalf of others or each other. You need each other.

When upset, however, neither one of you listens to the other. Together you can become paranoid, both expecting the worst. Your dwelling on situations or others is really a waste of your energy.

a white with a white

...supplies the freedom each needs to do what they want in life. This gives you the power to stay focused on your future without interference.

When there is a crisis, you both need space. One of you must struggle to bring the relationship back on track. Your conversations can become overly focused on making changes instead of appreciating what you have. You both have lives apart from each other.

a brown with a brown

...creates a world all their own when they first meet. You both seem to make work fun or life a more comfortable place to be. Your concerns are about where you live and what you are doing. You become delightfully lost in the pleasures of the moment.

In a crisis, things come to a halt. You both need experiences apart from each other to recharge your batteries. Your friends regenerate you.

a black with a white

...makes good decisions. As a black, you talk about your feelings. This makes a white more comfortable with his or her own emotions, and more secure. The white's objectivity calms your emotions, giving you the ability to see new options, to look around before you leap.

In a crisis, as a white, your objectivity can make the black view you as cold and uncaring. The black will become more aggressive, trying to get even closer to you. You then feel closed in, viewing the black as being too needy, and back off even more. The result is a clash, good conversation, or great sex.

a black with a brown

...creates passion. As a black, you challenge a brown by questioning them about what they are getting out of life. This can encourage the brown to accumulate more wealth or see more value in the relationship. A brown keeps you from hitting brick walls. The brown's intuitiveness teaches you to come back down to earth and concentrate on current practicalities, not past emotions.

In a crisis, a black can discount the value of experiencing things. As a brown, you can become wounded, which makes you feel less important and not appreciated. You can become consumed with what you are doing, causing the black to feel like they are simply an afterthought in your life.

a white with a brown

...discovers new possibilities to enjoy. As a white, you help a brown move forward in his or her relationships and career by making constant suggestions. The brown's ability to maintain steadfast relationships allows you to feel closer to the people around you.

As a brown, your dedication can be seen as somewhat limited thinking to a white. When you do not feel appreciated, you start helping others who need you. The white can feel discarded, as if you don't notice they are around. In disassociating from the white, you turn them on. They have an entirely new appreciation of your contribution.

YOUR ACHROMATIC BOUNDARIES

Your need for personal space creates emotional boundaries. When someone stands back too far, you feel that they have left you. If they get too close, you can feel that they are imposing on you. This continual back and forth game of creating distance one moment and being uncomfortably close the next is life's struggle to be intimate with someone yet not lose yourself.

CHOOSE YOUR FAVORITE ACHROMATIC COLOR BETWEEN ONLY BLACK AND WHITE. YOU WILL LEARN HOW YOU ARE GIVING UP YOUR PERSONAL SPACE.

IF YOU PREFER BLACK, you push forward. Your emotions make others feel your presence. This can irritate or stimulate the other person. You create an intense feeling of closeness by eliminating emotional distance. Being closer makes your relationship more intimate.

IF YOU PREFER WHITE, you step back to preserve your space and maintain your objectivity. This motivates the intimacy-seeking blacks to move closer. This seesaw movement creates exciting energy. It stimulates new thoughts and feelings.

WHEN YOU BOTH LIKE BLACK OR WHITE, things get a bit crazy. If both of you like black, one is forced outside of their comfort zone. They must become distant and more objective, like a white. The reverse is also true. If both of you like white, one is forced outside of their comfort zone to become closer, more intimate like a black.

laughing out loud

Awareness of nonverbal communication is not only essential—it's fun! Play a spatial boundary game with your friends or partner to see what I mean. The only rule is to do the opposite of what you normally do. Then, watch as the other person becomes uncomfortable.

IF YOU PREFER BLACK, create spatial distance by standing away, and being more objective. Watch your friend become warmer or your partner become more lovey-dovey.

IF YOU PREFER WHITE, stand closer than normal and be more emotional. Watch your friend or partner become more objective, less emotional.

Your friend or partner will unconsciously assume your normal role, and chances are they won't like it at all. Afterwards, tell them what you have done. Understanding this powerful, nonverbal communication will strengthen your relationships and get a lot of laughs. You will become aware of the glue that keeps you both together.

HOW COLOR LANGUAGE EVOLVED

black is feeling emotion

Black is the absence of light. Close your eyes and your awareness will go inward to feel your past. In the darkness, your thoughts consider what or who has been important to you. You gain the power to know your feelings and gauge the value of each person or situation.

white is seeing options

White is light itself. Light gives you knowledge of the world around you. It gives you the freedom to rise beyond yourself or a situation to see new information. You gain the power to objectively view new options for your future.

brown is realizing authenticity

Brown is the earthy existence of the flesh. In accepting, not fabricating, the bold realities of each person or situation, you see their authenticity. You gain the power to see the far-reaching implications of each action or decision.

WHEN YOUR ACHROMATIC COLORS CHANGE

Should you find yourself drawn to a new achromatic color, you are questioning the very core of your existence. When your favorite achromatic color changes, you will feel indecisive, as if you are on shaky ground. A change in your least favorite achromatic color shows you are reevaluating your entire perspective on life.

THE ACHROMATIC IQ
ANSWER TRUE OR FALSE

black favorite achromatic color
1. Hangs on in a relationship till they drop.   T or F
2. Is never emotional.   T or F

black least favorite achromatic color
3. Is not the person to whom you should exaggerate.   T or F
4. At decision time is concerned with how you feel.   T or F

brown favorite achromatic color
5. Can sometimes be seen as insincere.   T or F
6. Can become stubborn if they want something.   T or F

brown least favorite achromatic color
7. Loves to tell you how old they are.   T or F
8. Can be a virgin and tell you how to have great sex.   T or F

white favorite achromatic color
9. Coined the phrase "I need space."   T or F
10. Sees freedom as no big thing.   T or F

white least favorite achromatic color
11. Panics when there is emotional change.   T or F
12. Doesn't care if they fit in.   T or F

★ Answers on the next page

ANSWERS TO THE ACHROMATIC QUIZ

black favorite achromatic color
1. T   Saying good-bye is a dramatic event.
2. F   Feelings direct their lives.

black least favorite achromatic color
3. T   Your drama will be a joke to them.
4. F   Once the decision is final they're cold.

brown favorite achromatic color
5. F   They're the real McCoy.
6. T   They never outgrew the terrible twos.

brown least favorite achromatic color
7. F   If they're over 30, don't even ask.
8. T   They don't acknowledge that you need to experience it before you understand it.

white favorite achromatic color
9. T   Close to them isn't that close.
10. F   It's everything.

white least favorite achromatic color
11. T   They freeze. Only later will they talk about it.
12. F   They make everything fit—even if it doesn't.

9 chapter

YOUR ENERGY TYPE

How you impact others is how they perceive you. In fulfilling yourself, you emit your passions. Make your primary, secondary, and achromatic color selections from pages 22 and 23.

COMBINE YOUR FAVORITE PRIMARY, SECONDARY,
AND ACHROMATIC COLORS TO GET YOUR ENERGY TYPE.

IN THIS CHAPTER

YOU WILL LEARN HOW OTHERS PERCEIVE YOU. Keep in mind this is not necessarily who you think you are.

READ YOUR ENERGY TYPE WITH A FRIEND. Many times their comments will give you a clearer view of yourself.

HOW MANY OF ME ARE THERE?

Within a sample population of approximately 4,000, read where your energy type ranked. The higher you rank, the more you are understood.

1. Blue Green White	10. Blue Purple Brown	19. Red Purple Brown
2. Blue Purple Black	11. Yellow Green White	20. Yellow Purple Brown
3. Blue Green Black	12. Yellow Purple Black	21. Blue Orange White
4. Blue Green Brown	13. Red Green Brown	22. Yellow Green Brown
5. Red Purple Black	14. Red Purple White	23. Yellow Orange Black
6. Blue Purple White	15. Yellow Green Black	24. Blue Orange Brown
7. Red Green Black	16. Yellow Orange White	25. Yellow Orange Brown
8. Red Green White	17. Red Orange Black	26. Red Orange Brown
9. Yellow Purple White	18. Blue Orange Black	27. Red Orange White

THE TRUTH SEEKERS

discover yourself

You are constantly reexamining yourself to identify what is important. Being truthful is your purpose in life. You need veracity to be aware of yourself. You will speak the truth even when others do not want to listen. When you first meet someone, they have no idea that this is who you are. After listening to them, you can't help but be open and honest. You stun them with your obvious truths.

dive in

If you make up your mind about something, there is nothing that can stop you from achieving your goals. You are able to remain focused and resourceful at the same time. By maintaining a keen awareness, you know what is working. This is your great talent. Concentrate on building a trusting rapport with others instead of dwelling on how you are different. Others will feel secure with the advice that you give them and you will be able to recognize your own emotional patterns in the future.

but beware

When people are unwilling to listen, they may reject your ideas or avoid you. Don't feel that you're misunderstood or that you're an outcast. Others are just trying to protect themselves. Accept that you are someone who must tell the truth and that many times others are not strong enough to confront the realities you reveal.

relationship tips

Your intense, high-energy personality is somewhat hidden in a crowd. Strangers will see you as honest and open. You need a cause and you usually find it in being there for someone.

IF YOU CHOOSE BLUE AS YOUR LEAST FAVORITE PRIMARY, you are dedicated to giving support to the people in your life who really need you. You are a great friend. Your objective opinions are remarkably accurate. In fact, they can shock those around you so forcefully that they fail to see how much you care. Before you express yourself, tell others, "I have a thought that might help." They will then be better able to understand the way you show love.

IF YOU CHOOSE RED AS YOUR LEAST FAVORITE PRIMARY, you are seeking to be respected. At first you hide who you are, then suddenly reveal yourself to others as a strong, opinionated person they had no idea existed. You are a character! Even though your truthful, well thought out statements need to be uttered, you become overly sensitive when others frown at your remarks. Direct your truths at those who are really available to listen. Their positive response will give you the respect that you deserve.

work tips

You need to be respected as an authority at whatever you do. Use your directness to educate people on how to perform their jobs better and to increase productivity. When others realize you have their best interests at heart, they will respect your talents. You're at your best when you are regularly securing new and better worlds for those around you. Jobs such as residential architect, real estate broker, doctor, nurse, or counselor will make you feel more complete.

things will be just fine if

...prior to giving advice, you consider whether the other person is in the frame of mind to listen. If not, stop talking. Make a mental note and try having the conversation at another time, using a less emotional way of making your point. Eventually, you will be heard and the truth will come out.

yellow, green and black

THE DESIGNERS

discover yourself

You create new ways of improving environments. Your awareness of others and your surroundings allows you to assemble better supportive structures. You design new systems and ways of bettering work or living situations.

An environment with fewer rules will give you the flexibility to see new perspectives. In this world, you can identify each item or resource in your surroundings that makes you or others more comfortable. You will feel that burst of spiritual freedom you are seeking.

dive in

You enjoy assessing the environment, and look for the best options. Since you do not form opinions easily, you often change your point of view and modify your goals with each step of a task. Take advantage of your flexibility to change as situations evolve. Make your fact-based suggestions work.

but beware

You sense when others are in the mood to hear what needs to be said. This is a talent. Why bother talking to someone who is not going to listen? Knowing when you are being listened to allows you to make changes in even the most difficult situations or with the most stubborn people.

relationship tips

You are a very flexible, sensitive lover, friend, or parent. You are very considerate. You will not rest until you know that everyone around you is okay. Make sure you tell people what you need. Otherwise, you may feel as though you're doing for everyone else and getting nothing back.

IF YOU CHOOSE BLUE AS YOUR LEAST FAVORITE PRIMARY, your emotional commitment to others pulls your life together. You have an amazing ability to see what others need to make their lives work. This is your great contribution. Take a close look at what you gain from your various interactions. You'll see how you are progressing in your relationships. You will become closer to those you love.

IF YOU CHOOSE RED AS YOUR LEAST FAVORITE PRIMARY, your lack of directness can hide the real you, making it very difficult for others to know how to support you. When you are being supportive of others, make sure that you tell them what you need, as well. You and everyone else will feel more important.

work tips

Your communication skills are a tremendous asset in today's work force. You understand the other person's perspective. Adopting their viewpoint helps you express your thoughts diplomatically. You help others appreciate new approaches and different possibilities. This tears down barriers.

When you're at your best, you bring respect for the individual and a sense of integrity to the conversation. Jobs like interior decorator, real estate agent, career counselor, programmer, travel agent, or any job where you can recommend how to construct a more supportive world would be best for you.

things will be just fine if

...you stop always considering what else others need and focus, instead, on what you need.

yellow, green and white

THE GIVERS

discover yourself

You have a tremendous capacity to experience different people and situations and make them part of your own psyche. By recognizing where there's a need for greater balance, you become aware of what others need to exist. This makes it easy for you to create nurturing environments that allow for you and others to live more in the moment and feel more alive.

Your support heals and grounds others, enabling them to be open to your insights about what they need. In turn, this allows them to be themselves. Your very essence is to be needed and to give to others a better world in which to live. Through giving to others you heal yourself.

dive in

Use your highly realistic perspective to learn how to improve your environment. Recognize the needs of others by studying their actions. Tell them what is necessary for them to do. Your quiet strength allows others to trust you and to let you know who they are. This gives you the ability to recommend things to them. You are recognized as a very giving person, even though you probably don't think so.

but beware

If you feel that you are being selfish, you are not in an environment that is supportive of your abilities. Don't be a victim. Get tough with people who do not appreciate you. Show them how much you do. Your hard work must command respect. Otherwise, you will burn out, become defensive, and hide all the love and concern that you have to give.

relationship tips

TO UNDERSTAND YOUR ENERGY IN A RELATIONSHIP YOU NEED TO SELECT ANOTHER ACHROMATIC COLOR. Do you prefer black or white?

If you prefer black, you're a yellow-green-black. If you prefer white, you're a yellow-green-white. Now, read the relationship tips in yellow-green-black or yellow-green-white found in this chapter to see who you are in your relationships.

work tips

Dedication allows you to direct and focus your energy. But you'll get ahead in your career only if you are allowed to be important. Recognition gives you the strength to know how to fix things and give support even before others ask for it. Action-oriented jobs where you can be an expert, such as a doctor, nurse, physical therapist, or chiropractor, are ones you would enjoy. The more you are needed, the more fun your job will be.

things will be just fine if

...you accept that you have a great need to be appreciated. Direct your concerns to those who care about you. Only then will you be able to acknowledge and take more pride in what you contribute.

yellow, green and brown

THE FACILITATORS

yellow, purple and black

discover yourself

You seek to know about spiritual values to understand better the meaning of life and create a sense of purpose. You analyze each feeling you encounter and try to envision possibilities. Your intense interest allows you to focus on getting things done.

Your strong intuitive nature also gives you the ability to understand what others need to grow. You judge people by the quality of their hearts and their spiritual potential, not their possessions or status. You create an understanding of the inner self.

dive in

You have the power to inspire. Be yourself. Without even knowing it, you will entice others to find their spiritual selves. Your concern paves the way for them to feel secure enough to explore their interests.

but beware

At times, your intensity towards personal growth can actually impede your progress. Intensity works better when it is directed outward, not inward. Don't let guilt-ridden thoughts deplete your energy. Set emotional boundaries that protect you from becoming too immersed in yourself or in other people's situations. Compulsive concerns can be a defense used to avoid your own problems.

relationship tips

TO VIEW YOUR ENERGY IN A RELATIONSHIP, YOU NEED TO SELECT ANOTHER COLOR. Do you prefer blue, red, green, or orange?

If you prefer blue, you're a blue-purple-black. Red, you're a red-purple-black. Green, you're a yellow-green-black. Orange, you're a yellow-orange-black. Now, turn to that energy type in this chapter and read who you are in your relationships.

work tips

Your investigative, focused personality gives you the opportunity to be an expert in your chosen field. You desire to experience and analyze. Learning is your motivation, not money. Doing and experiencing new things means everything to you.

And yes, you are a people person. You can regenerate yourself and allow others to be the gems that they are. A few careers that will work for you are doctor, lawyer, judge, or data analyzer.

things will be just fine if

...you recognize, for the most part, where your actions are repeating routines, and you are simply viewing the same thing over and over from a different point of view. This will give you a clear perspective of yourself.

yellow, purple and black

THE SPIRITUAL WIZARDS

discover yourself

You are on a journey to investigate who and what really matters in your life. In the beginning, everything seems to work. After a while, though, you are better able to recognize the focal point of your passions. Then you begin to question if you might be happier elsewhere, with different people or in different situations.

You are steadily trying to balance yourself by seeking new options for your spirit. New things allow you to express your inner energy. You like to do lots of things to see how it feels. You are having fun when your environment is changing all the time. Isn't this how you create more passion in your relationships and situations?

dive in

You know what people need in order to grow. Be the inspiring force that you are and make suggestions for others to improve their lives. Create better reasons to learn and live, as well as new spiritual perspectives that help you see hidden truths. Use your excellent communication skills to empower others to make their lives more genuine. Be the spiritual wizard that this world so dearly needs.

but beware

Forever pondering what to do can hinder your growth. You can become so busy that you lose your ability to set priorities for yourself. Your world can seem to fall apart.

Trust your own beliefs about what would improve things. You'll find that you are usually right. Don't get distracted. Your power for making suggestions about how to create inner passion is too vital not to be unleashed.

yellow, purple and white

relationship tips

TO VIEW YOUR ENERGY IN A RELATIONSHIP, YOU NEED TO SELECT ANOTHER COLOR. Do you prefer blue, red, green, or orange?

If you prefer blue, you're a blue-purple-white. Red, you're a red-purple-white. Green, you're a yellow-green-white. Orange, you're a yellow-orange-white. Now, turn to that energy type in this chapter and read who you are in your relationships.

work tips

Your career decisions are based on personal growth. You focus on how much you are going to learn. You prefer non-repetitive jobs where you are always being asked to see fresh perspectives. New things energize you. They reinforce your confidence.

You can do almost any job that involves constant change. Fast-growing companies and project-oriented settings where no workday resembles the one before will turn you on. You need to respect the people for whom you work. After all, you must believe in someone before you can learn from him or her.

things will be just fine if

...you celebrate personal victories. Acknowledge how you have allowed others to be more passionate. Your personal power will become even greater. You will see exactly who you are and you will understand how to regenerate your own passion.

yellow, purple and white

THE SHAMANS

discover yourself
Knowing what you want and when you want it gives you spiritual freedom. It fuels your desire to heal yourself and others. Expressing passion gives your spirit the ability to rebuild a wounded soul.

You are aware of the spiritual energy around you. You touch people in a profound, life-altering way. Without anyone's suspecting it, you give him or her the awareness to declare their inner passions. You're a spiritual healer.

dive in
Encourage situations that are positive. Use your power to identify and eliminate those that are not. It may be as simple as recognizing who is having fun and who is not, or asking the right questions to help everyone understand what's going on.

Very few have the level of awareness that you do. So warn people who are in jeopardy of losing their passions, and help them mend things before it's too late.

but beware
Your need to experience life at such a high volume makes it difficult for others to notice your merits. They may feel your advice is too personal and not be able to hear what you have to say.

Remind yourself about your contributions and recognize what you accomplish with every action you take. Otherwise, you will lose your motivation and it will be difficult to complete important things. Your kind, giving nature is too valuable to be hidden deep inside of you.

relationship tips

TO VIEW YOUR ENERGY IN A RELATIONSHIP, YOU FIRST NEED TO SELECT ANOTHER COLOR. Do you prefer blue, red, green, or orange?

If you prefer blue, you're a blue-purple. Red, you're a red-purple. Green, you're a yellow-green. Orange, you're a yellow-orange.

NOW, YOU NEED TO SELECT ANOTHER ACHROMATIC COLOR. Do you prefer black or white?

If you prefer black, add this new color to what you learned above to become a blue-purple-black, red-purple-black, yellow-green-black, or a yellow-orange-black. If you prefer white, you become a blue-purple-white, red-purple-white, yellow-green-white, or a yellow-orange-white. Now, turn to your new energy type in this chapter and read about your relationships.

work tips

Choose an environment where you can do your own thing in conjunction with someone else. You gravitate toward people who will teach you through new experiences. You know opportunity when you see it. Experiencing new situations is a thrill. They enable you to learn how to fit better into the world around you.

Take advantage of your ability to make things work. You will enjoy high activity professions where you are part of a team or participate in expansive technologies like computer systems.

things will be just fine if

...you tell those you care about how dedicated you are to them. Doing for others is not enough. They must hear about your feelings in your own words. Your friends will then remind you of how much you give to them. This will regenerate your spirit.

THE INVENTORS

discover yourself

You are able to shape your varied experiences into something cohesive. Technical information and diverse projects are pooled together and are used for future inventions. You have the unusual combination of being able to work with both people and things. You enjoy living fast, but you slow down to process information and make long-term decisions. This change in gears helps you get what you want.

dive in

You're an innovator, far ahead of anyone else with both people and projects. You have the ability to create something from nothing by reinventing the resources around you. When your thinking is direct and intense, new ideas and possibilities arrive with a bang. Set your mind on something and nothing will stop you. Your know-how is unparalleled.

but beware

When people first meet you, they are not aware of your warmth. Instead, they get caught up in your defenses. Once they see the personable, vulnerable you, they will become aware of your needs and will feel important.

relationship tips

Your exciting, magnetic persona is hard to ignore when you enter a room. You are a very inventive and fun person. Others get to know your sensitive side by your efforts in their behalf. You create liveliness where it is needed. You especially enjoy turning the most boring situation or mundane routine into a party. When you create positive change, you're at your best.

IF YOU CHOOSE BLUE AS YOUR LEAST FAVORITE PRIMARY COLOR, your commitment to change pulls your life together. You use your on and off speeds to set boundaries. This allows you to protect your heart. Be careful. When you become overconcerned with your thoughts, you can lose your power to see the big picture.

IF YOU CHOOSE RED AS YOUR LEAST FAVORITE PRIMARY COLOR, you are seeking respect. Though initially you hide who you are, soon others are suddenly confronted by a strong individual they had no idea existed. You are an enigma. Despite all your achievements, you can feel wounded if others frown at your boldness. Direct your energy toward people who care enough to listen to you. Their positive responses and respect are what you deserve.

work tips

Use your abilities to encourage people and construct new things by pulling together the resources and talents around you. You are a natural at technical work. You're also a great motivator of people. Use both these talents and you will feel complete. Your people skills and technical abilities accommodate a wide range of careers.

things will be just fine if

...you stop going through life with a ready-made checklist. Otherwise, even those you love will perceive themselves as unimportant, merely items on a long grocery list.

yellow, orange and black

THE INFORMATION JUNKIES

discover yourself

You seek information to gain self-recognition. You take things apart to analyze how they are made, and then wonder why they weren't made another way. You try to concentrate on learning pertinent facts and are aware that what is now in vogue will eventually become dated. This appreciation keeps you on the cusp. You are the first to know the latest information.

You are the lightest color combination and the most undefined in the entire color spectrum. You easily become a part of any situation. You mold your behavior to fit those around you. Without conflict and barriers, you can receive more information.

dive in

Observe the options and resources available. Your methodical way of analyzing facts is your great talent. Continually making suggestions about available options, you can concentrate on the facts regardless of life's pressures. Your knowledge makes everyone's life easier to endure, less emotionally erratic, and more about what is important.

but beware

Don't get caught up in making plans and agendas and then fail to act on them. When you get too intense and are overloaded with information it becomes difficult for you to think clearly. Others can see you as not having a clear focus in life.

relationship tips

Your energetic, vivacious, and inquisitive personality is tuned in to everyone around you. You offer outrageous solutions that often work. When uncomfortable, however, you give too much information. Talk less and your invaluable advice will gain you the recognition you are seeking.

IF YOU CHOOSE BLUE AS YOUR LEAST FAVORITE PRIMARY COLOR, your dedication to others pulls your life together and helps you see what they need to improve their lives. This is a great talent. Try to be mindful of what you give. Appreciating yourself will make you closer to those you love.

IF YOU CHOOSE RED AS YOUR LEAST FAVORITE PRIMARY COLOR, you have a great need to be respected by your peers. But don't put on airs or hide behind knowledge to try to impress people. You'll make it difficult for people to appreciate you for what you have to say. When you are giving advice to others, try not to neglect your own feelings. The more sincere you are, the closer your relationships will be.

work tips

By analyzing numbers and information, you know whether or not something will work. You'll thrive at jobs where you can rely on your factual expertise. Consider working with computers, research, or being a librarian.

Don't be subtle when correcting co-workers or giving them instructions. Being firm will help them see why things have to be done a certain way. Only after they have spent time around you will they get used to your low-key criticism.

things will be just fine if

...you dwell longer on the nuances that you are considering. Otherwise, in your quest for new information, you'll become lost in all the details.

yellow, orange and white

yellow, orange and brown

THE TROUBLESHOOTERS

discover yourself

You're the one who makes sure that everything is working, whether it has to do with the lives of friends or with something mechanical, such as a noisy engine. You have the ability to see the needs of others and understand just what you are capable of doing to help. When you are committed and loyal to someone, you help him or her recognize their strengths.

dive in

You have the ability to create a world where others can have more passion. Your high energy level and intense living style wakes up even the dullest moments. You're a perfect example of how to live.

Use your ability to see how things work to regenerate your relationships and situations. Focus on how everything fits together. You will give others a better understanding of their everyday processes and increase their ability to enjoy the individual moments of their lives. This fresh perspective is your forte.

but beware

Guard against becoming too immersed in what you are doing. If you lose sight of your objective, you will lose your creativity and yourself. Hold on to your future by staying committed to your overall plan. Don't sound the fire alarm when you intuitively know the negative actions of others. Allow them more time. People are simply not as aware of the significance of their actions as you are.

relationship tips

TO VIEW YOUR ENERGY IN A RELATIONSHIP, YOU NEED TO SELECT ANOTHER ACHROMATIC COLOR. Do you prefer black or white?

If you prefer black, you're a yellow-orange-black; if white, you're a yellow-orange-white. Now, read the relationship tips in yellow-orange-black or yellow-orange-white found in this chapter to see how you are in your relationships.

work tips

You clearly understand people's contributions. Use your ability to recognize the doers from the talkers. No matter how anyone tries to get the emotional edge on you, that's not going to happen. Use your exactness to ensure that the facts are the primary consideration.

You'll thrive at jobs that allow you to concentrate on the nuts and bolts and to fix things. Avoid work environments where you're forced to deal with abstract concepts.

things will be just fine if

...you make people aware of your accomplishments. This will help you to see who really believes in your abilities. Otherwise, your dedication can falter and you can lose focus.

yellow, orange and brown

THE IDENTITY CREATORS

discover yourself

You are in touch with your emotions and clearly express what you want. When you listen to the concerns of others, you discover what is best for them. You help them accept themselves. They learn about things that they have deeply internalized and are afraid to face. You strengthen their identity. You give to others the gift of better knowing who they are.

dive in

You can hear others' hopes and fears by their tone of voice. Engage others in conversation so that you can help them dis-cover what they need. Take your concerns and translate them into supportive suggestions. Keeping each person or situation on track is your greatest talent. It allows you to distinguish your own identity as well.

but beware

You have a great need for others to hear you as well as you hear them. If you become frustrated, you ask others questions about decisions that you've already made. In your search to confirm your feelings, people can feel that you're uninterested in their comments. They perceive you are not listening to what they say. You do hear them. It just takes you longer to process information about your feelings.

relationship tips

Your attractive, attentive appearance is very alluring. Your puppy-dog eyes express real concern. You love to be doted on. Your thoughts are about being supported or supporting others. This makes you a natural in relationships. You have a sincere love for those around you. This is one of your greatest powers.

IF YOU CHOOSE YELLOW AS YOUR LEAST FAVORITE PRIMARY COLOR, you see others as who they believe themselves to be. Beware. You can attract someone who does not respect your concerns. Don't be so stubborn. Make sure your expectations are realistic before you set your heart on them.

IF YOU CHOOSE RED AS YOUR LEAST FAVORITE PRIMARY COLOR, you appear very vulnerable. This gives you the power to be very seductive. Others have a need to give you whatever you want. The problem is that they do not have a clue about you, let alone what you really want. Speak up more.

work tips

Be sensitive to the emotions of your co-workers and be supportive. This is a responsibility that you rightly claim. If you are a manager, appreciate your ability to remain dedicated to your staff and you will gain strong employee commitment and loyalty. Be careful. If you get too close to those you work with, you will be unable to give unbiased guidance. You work best in environments where you are consistently working with new clients or situations.

Careers that allow you to hear and express how others feel are a must for you. Working as a writer, actor, psychologist, psychiatrist, manager, or designer of support systems will allow you to use your natural talents.

things will be just fine if

…you stop compulsively talking about or considering what is not working for you. Dwelling on non-supportive situations or relationships too long can stop you from moving forward.

blue, green and black

THE INTELLECTUALS

blue, green and white

discover yourself

Your objective point of view helps people to understand what they need to have a more balanced life. Your straightforward, unbiased comments make it easy for others to hear you. They understand that you're genuinely motivated to make their lives better. Improving the status quo sparks your inner passion.

dive in

You have astute common sense, even in difficult situations where others lose their cool. By staying concerned and objective, you have the power to recommend solutions. This is your natural talent. You can keep your distance, yet maintain your concern. People's faith in you gives you the inner strength to believe more in yourself.

but beware

When you're upset you put distance between yourself and those who rely on you. This can make you seem aloof, and people may start to question whether you believe in them. If you don't let others know who you are and how you feel, they will become remote and feel unimportant. You can drive away people who treasure, love, and support you the most.

relationship tips

You get others interested by giving them your undivided attention. Then you appear unavailable. Some might find this enticing, but it will be difficult for them to get close to you. Intimacy can make you uncomfortable after a while. You require information.

IF YOU CHOOSE YELLOW AS YOUR LEAST FAVORITE PRIMARY COLOR, you appear to be very open and endearing. Others can feel that you have a need to be loved. Then, you become unavailable. Aren't you logically justifying whether or not the relationship is of value to you? Be careful. Keep your concerns focused on those you love.

IF YOU CHOOSE RED AS YOUR LEAST FAVORITE PRIMARY COLOR, others see you as very mysterious and flirtatious. Initially you enjoy mental stimulation. However, you can find yourself in relationships where there is very little physical chemistry. Your emotions can be saying yes, while you are thinking no. If there's sexual attraction, there is real potential for a solid relationship. You will still be curious about all the options available. Who else would you like to be with? How would it feel?

work tips

You are at your best when you are recommending easier ways of doing things. You don't become obsessed with the need to realize the final goal. Your neutral perspective enables you to teach, perform managerial duties, or work for large corporations.

things will be just fine if

...you communicate your need for space, then take the time to discern which relationships and situations are vital to you.

blue, green and white

THE DREAM MAKERS

discover yourself

You experience a sense of personal harmony when you help people. Your capacity to listen and offer suggestions allows them to become more aware of what they need. They gain a balanced perspective. You avoid extremes and use facts to improve situations. You know how to make others' dreams come true by taking the appropriate action.

dive in

Your clear understanding of the needs of people gives you a realistic approach to your relationships and your environment. Use your natural talent to promote people and causes. Take on other people's burdens as if they were your own. You will create new worlds that benefit everyone. You are the dream maker.

but beware

In a crisis where things can be overwhelming, you become overly concerned with what others need. You end up feeling deprived and overreact by doing what you want to do regardless of what is expected. This can lead to your destroying things that later you will miss. Being too nice and then too selfish can make it difficult for others to appreciate all the good you do.

relationship tips

TO UNDERSTAND YOUR BEHAVIOR IN A RELATIONSHIP, YOU NEED TO SELECT ANOTHER ACHROMATIC COLOR. Do you prefer black or white?

If you prefer black, you're a blue-green-black. White, you're a blue-green-white. Now, read the relationship tips in blue-green-black or blue-green-white found in this chapter to see how you are in your relationships.

work tips

The more you participate, the more fun your job will be. You enjoy creating environments that allow others to be hopeful about the future. Acknowledge your ability to perform tasks. Act with positive energy. People will feel your inner fire and be motivated to act.

You are at your best when you are supporting people through periods of crisis or fixing things. You see life from a physical, supportive perspective. You'd enjoy working as a doctor, nurse, physical therapist, corporate trainer, chiropractor, or carpenter.

things will be just fine if

...you stop being so dedicated to others and tell them what you need. Your life will become fun again.

blue, green and brown

THE PIONEERS

discover yourself

You think about why people do what they do. By understanding the motivation of others, you seek to create a better world. Changing the world around you through personal achievements is your everyday challenge. The constant investigation of feelings, thoughts, and ideas is your passion.

dive in

You are the darkest color in the spectrum. Darkness denotes emotional depth. Use your talents to visualize possibilities. Your ability to picture things clearly in your head helps you perform tasks with very few missteps and minimal risk. Others see this quality as self-confidence. They think you always know what you are doing. Stay focused on the big picture. When you understand the overall concept there's nothing you can't do.

but beware

You will not be able to accomplish things exactly the way you envision them. Be realistic and realize that every process must be constantly revamped and adapted. When you feel emotional about something, stop and take a breath. Chances are you are ignoring concrete facts or items. Have you made unrealistic assumptions? Do you see an easier way? No, you can't have everything you expected, but you can have most of it.

relationship tips

The romantic ideas in your head make the world around you delicious. You need to be enveloped by your lover. Forget the practical details. Surreal is more fun.

IF YOU CHOOSE YELLOW AS YOUR LEAST FAVORITE PRIMARY COLOR, your dramatic, eccentric flair is sexy. The only problem is that many times you move too fast, and get what you think you want instead of what you really need. Be more cautious and realistic about other people before you get involved. Otherwise, you will be constantly disappointed.

IF YOU CHOOSE RED AS YOUR LEAST FAVORITE PRIMARY COLOR, you see the depth and possibilities of each person. This makes you very appealing. You're open to everything. Others love your fun and easy-going style. However, your openness can make you vulnerable. Loving and caring about someone is not about ignoring your own needs. Make a list of things you require. Whenever someone or something fails to meet a criterion, talk about it.

work tips

Use your big-picture thinking to develop new markets, new ideas, and new businesses. You see what is missing and know what is required to get things done. You are a great motivator who needs to make an impact and express new ideas. Your dramatic flare helps initiate action. Creative fields such as advertising, marketing, sales, design, trial law, or any area that allows you to investigate the unknown will make you the happiest.

things will be just fine if

...you stop thinking so much. Your obsession with your ideas or planning the way you are going to feel can make it difficult for you to enjoy the day.

THE PROBLEM SOLVERS

discover yourself

You are constantly considering what else each person or situation requires. You want to know what is missing. During this period of mulling things over, others might view you as passive or quiet. When you have assembled all the facts about the situation, you lean forward with a vibrant suggestion on how to make something or someone's life work better. Solving problems is your greatest passion.

dive in

Examine ideas and situations. Tell others about better ways to solve a problem. Be steadfast. Your method of forcing yourself to work under pressure allows you to be at your best. You can see the idea and critique it until it is perfect. Demand autonomy. You need it to finish what you start. A sharp, successful focus will be your reward.

but beware

When you don't know what you want, you can appear wishy-washy to others. It can also make it difficult for you to stay focused. External pressure can destroy your ability to concentrate and be creative.

Make your own plan and take the time to weigh all the options. In order to give yourself some thinking space for problem solving, tell others you will have to get back to them. Later, you can let them know your thoughts on how to resolve difficulties.

blue, purple and white

relationship tips

Your classy style creates romantic possibilities. When you first meet a person, you have no clue if they are right for you. Only when you spend time with them alone will you know if they fit your ideal.

IF YOU CHOOSE YELLOW AS YOUR LEAST FAVORITE PRIMARY COLOR, your need to know all the answers can make you appear unavailable or somewhat formal. Then, all of a sudden others may see you as a very open person. Enjoy the present, instead of obsessing over the future. Others will see your warmth. Who or what you are looking for will appear.

IF YOU CHOOSE RED AS YOUR LEAST FAVORITE PRIMARY COLOR, you appear seductive and intriguing, even forbidden. Others will find you very appealing, and may even be surprised when later on they see how logical you are. Express your feelings, not just your thoughts. Otherwise, you will waste a lot of time and create a lot of frustration.

work tips

Analyze your options and use your creativity to transform ideas into reality. Request that you learn why everyone did each task. This will allow your logical mind to fit everything together. You are good at organizing, developing, and creating things. However, too many ideas, agendas, or different topics can make you scattered.

Your advice gives others new perspectives on how to create a better future. You would excel at such jobs as career counseling, public relations, human resources, corporate law, or architecture.

things will be just fine if

...you give yourself the space and time to connect your thoughts. Initially your thinking is rigid, then flexible. On your own you can weave both of these tendencies into a comprehensive plan.

blue, purple and white

THE SCIENTIFIC THINKERS

blue, purple and brown

discover yourself

You hypothesize possibilities. Then you measure them. You passionately investigate new methods to see what works. Your inquisitiveness and methodical approach help you to gain insight into the future of your relationships and situations.

Your keen awareness and belief that things will work out give you the dedication to do things in a more thorough way. You recognize, even before things begin, where you can make improvements. You are constantly moving forward with your feet on the ground to create a better world.

dive in

Be direct. Take action and improve the physical world. Use your compulsive need to search for practical solutions to develop even better methods for improving things. When you are dedicated to something, there is no stopping you. You become persistent and aware of each issue that needs to be addressed. Seeing what you have actually accomplished is a must for you.

but beware

You need to complete things or you will become disheartened. When this occurs, you can become too direct. Others can see you as rude. Don't deliberate for too long, rehashing the same old possibilities. Stay focused on your long-term goals and seek out environments that give you plenty of autonomy. If you don't keep busy doing constructive things, you will feel lost.

relationship tips

TO VIEW YOUR ENERGY IN A RELATIONSHIP, YOU NEED TO SELECT ANOTHER ACHROMATIC COLOR. Do you prefer black or white?

If you prefer black, you're a blue-purple-black. If you prefer white, you're a blue-purple-white. Now, read the relationship tips in blue-purple-black or blue-purple-white found in this chapter to see how you are in your relationships.

work tips

You have a very realistic understanding of how to get the job done. Your ability to envision new things and see if they work gives you the appearance of a truly calm, analytical, process-oriented person. Doing what you want allows you to create long-term plans.

A few occupations you might consider are research scientist, actor, quality control production manager, new product designer, or chef.

things will be just fine if

...you have the freedom to do what you enjoy. Your creations will be personal celebrations.

blue, purple and brown

THE MANAGERS

discover yourself

Your thoughts are about constructing something new. You are constantly looking at past experiences to see what was of value. Then you tell everyone what actions need to be taken or avoided. Keeping things on the right course is your greatest passion.

dive in

You're an expert at asking pertinent questions. They allow you and others to see what contributes to a situation. You can make people and resources fit together. Use your sharp perception to scrutinize what is important and you will be able to complete any task that you are given. You have a natural managerial style.

but beware

Don't let your intense scrutiny of things slow you down. Prioritize your plans for the future. It will free you of your past without so much effort. Others will find you more lovable and exciting. They will open up to you even more.

blue, orange and black

relationship tips

TO UNDERSTAND YOUR ENERGY IN A RELATIONSHIP, YOU NEED TO SELECT ANOTHER COLOR. Do you prefer yellow, red, green, or purple?

If you prefer yellow, you're a yellow-orange-black. Red, you're a red-orange-black. Green, you're a blue-green-black. Purple, you're a blue-purple-black. Now, turn to that energy type found in this chapter and read how you are in your relationships.

work tips

You direct a task by taking advantage of others' feedback. Your concerned questions make them respect you. You understand that developing something new requires their commitment. The information you derive allows you to better direct projects. You make sure that those who are loyal to you or your company are treated with respect. When you are focused, you are a natural leader.

You'll prefer a busy environment, even if there is stress involved, because you'll enjoy learning. Pressure actually stimulates you. Careers involving task management, overseeing change implementation, value assessment, and analyzing efficiency are best for you.

things will be just fine if

...you do not become overly engrossed in memories. You will gain a vision of how to build a future that provides better for your emotional needs.

blue, orange and black

THE SOCIAL INVESTIGATORS

discover yourself

You learn through watching others or by analyzing how things are made. When you watch others, you're drawn to their energy as if you were watching TV. You see each person's contribution. By examining their point of view, you see the very depths of their motivation. This is how you regularly fine-tune the way you direct your own life.

dive in

Use your excellent eye to examine closely just why your goals are not being realized. Your ability to view situations in great detail let's you see things that no one else could imagine. This is your great talent. You can initiate a plan or introduce something new, critique why it is or isn't working, then offer new perspectives and solutions.

but beware

The process of setting goals and analyzing them works better for you in your career than at home. You need to invent your own activities, as opposed to being told what to do. Without the freedom to explore your passions, you can get caught up in an endless cycle of second-guessing yourself. This is dangerous, because ultimately you'll wind up talking yourself out of what you really need.

relationship tips

TO UNDERSTAND YOUR ENERGY IN A RELATIONSHIP, YOU NEED TO SELECT ANOTHER COLOR. Do you prefer yellow, red, green, or purple?

If you prefer yellow, you're a yellow-orange-white. Red, you're a red-orange-white. Green, you're a blue-green-white. Purple, you're a blue-purple-white. Now, turn to that energy type found in this chapter and read about how you are in your relationships.

work tips

You have the power to construct new things in the workplace. You can both initiate change and asses what you have created. Effortlessly, you are able to decide how to direct resources and people. At the start, your strong beliefs make things work. If you get bored or distracted, however, you can lose your ability to complete projects successfully.

Your never-ending suggestions work well in busy jobs like the hospitality industry, corporate law, resource management, and employment recruitment.

things will be just fine if

...you slow down. Don't be such a fast thinker. Don't end a conversation until those around you have had the time to have their say. Give them the time to understand all the facts. They will be better able to assist you.

blue, orange and white

THE ACTIVISTS

discover yourself

You're well loved, giving, and affectionate. Maybe that's because you're dedicated to making the world a better place. You're not just a talker; you're a person of action. You introduce a sense of purpose and caring to your social environment. The activist in you brings people together to work toward improving the future. You have the ability to create hope.

dive in

Embrace your dedication to change the world around you. You are at your best when you are actually doing something that you helped plan. Your strong beliefs and no-nonsense approach make it happen. This style calms people down. It also allows them to believe in you. Your astute awareness is comforting.

but beware

When you're upset or under pressure you may do the wrong thing, even though it feels right at the time. Avoid making rash decisions. Take a moment to relax and have fun. Your inner strength will return. Otherwise, you'll end up betraying the beliefs you hold dear.

relationship tips

TO UNDERSTAND YOUR ENERGY IN A RELATIONSHIP, YOU FIRST NEED TO SELECT ANOTHER COLOR. Do you prefer yellow, red, green, or purple?

If you prefer yellow, you're a yellow-orange; red, a red-orange; green, a blue-green; and purple, you're a blue-purple.

NOW, YOU ALSO NEED TO SELECT ANOTHER ACHROMATIC COLOR. Do you prefer black or white?

If you prefer black, then you're a yellow-orange-black, red-orange-black, blue-green-black, or a blue-purple-black. If you prefer white, you're a yellow-orange-white, red-orange-white, blue-green-white, or a blue-purple-white. Now, turn to your new energy type found in this chapter and read how you are in your relationships.

work tips

When you are focused on building something, you are at your best. Occupations that allow you to make direct, exact requests like an engineer, builder, or developer of new programs, companies, or products will challenge you. Also consider jobs where you can make a difference such as a social worker, policeman, or a fireman. You need lots of activity directed at improving services for those around you in order to feel good about yourself.

things will be just fine if

...you resist instant gratification. The future that you envisioned will be yours.

blue, orange and brown

THE INVESTORS

discover yourself

By focusing on what others need, you learn the exact value and potential of each person in different situations. You instinctively know how motivated others are in supporting you. This helps you surround yourself with the right people.

Your generous nature gives you a feeling of security. It makes you feel comfortable and in control of your life. You know that a better future can be achieved only by investing in those people who respect you and in situations that have the capability to grow.

dive in

Appreciate your ability to understand practical realities. By being sensitive to how different people express their emotions, you display your greatest talent. You learn which situations are supportive and which are not. In fact, you'll see what others need even when they don't know themselves. You make them feel comfortable in your presence, even when they barely know you.

but beware

Under pressure you obsess over facts, concern yourself with small matters, and lose sight of the big picture. This makes you so skeptical that you lose perspective and think only about short-term plans. Without a sense of hope for your future, you become overly critical of yourself and situations. Others can see you as judgmental. Nothing is ever all right or all wrong.

relationship tips

TO UNDERSTAND YOUR ENERGY IN A RELATIONSHIP, YOU NEED TO SELECT ANOTHER COLOR. Do you prefer blue, yellow, purple, or orange?

If you prefer blue, you're a blue-green-black. Yellow, you're a yellow-green-black. Purple, you're a red-purple-black. Orange, you're a red-orange-black. Now, turn to that energy type found in this chapter and read how you are in your relationships.

work tips

Appreciate your ability to know when support is needed and where money can be best spent. If your educational background allows, you can excel in careers that place a high emphasis upon the correct use of resources.

Consider fields like finance, accounting, banking, manufacturing, property management, production, investment, money management, consulting, architecture, selling a product, or teaching personal development. You will do well wherever you can be nurturing and direct.

things will be just fine if

...you know that people recognize your kindness, concern, and accomplishments. You will find the respect and self-esteem you are seeking.

red, green and black

THE PRACTICAL WIZARDS

discover yourself

You understand what people need to do to be more practical in their lives. By keeping your distance, you are able to identify the best available resources. You're constantly conducting an investigation of how to better use money and cultivate talent. Then, much to your amazement, solutions seem to appear from nowhere. Your objective, practical perspective can turn a disaster into a rousing success.

dive in

You have the power to know what points of view, resources, and approaches are needed. Your practical thoughts and considerations make the best of what you have. You combine talents or information to attain goals. Use your ability to assess things critically and create powerful change in people's lives. Those who believe in you will gain new opportunities.

but beware

You send confusing messages to others. One moment they see you as a person who makes them feel very important, the next moment they feel that they are just a number. In your search for new options, people can sense that you have forgotten they were there for you. Help them to understand your need to take a step back in order to solve problems. It will keep them on your team while you sort out all the facts.

relationship tips

TO UNDERSTAND YOUR ENERGY IN A RELATIONSHIP, YOU NEED TO SELECT ANOTHER COLOR. Do you prefer blue, yellow, purple, or orange?

If you prefer blue, you're a blue-green-white; yellow, you're a yellow-green-white; purple, you're a red-purple-white; and orange, you're a red-orange-white. Now, turn to that energy type found in this chapter and read how you are in your relationships.

work tips

Your logical, supportive perspective is often in demand. You understand the underlying premise of things and work best when challenged by new points of view. Look for environments where you can come into contact with different types of people and situations.

Jobs that involve compilation of facts, such as training, career development, organization of tasks, auditing, or marketing will allow you to express your energy.

things will be just fine if

...you recognize the value of change. New experiences help bolster your self-esteem and give you the self-confidence to focus on what is right in your life.

THE CRUSADERS

discover yourself

You bring out the best in people. You help them accept their limitations and abilities. Giving them a good dose of reality keeps them grounded. Your crusade is to develop people's self-awareness and make their dreams a reality.

dive in

Use your high energy level to make many improvements in the course of a day. Once you know what you want, go get it! Turn everyday needs into causes to champion. You can be a little tornado. When you direct your energy inward you are a tower of strength. When you turn that energy toward others you are a giver; and toward goals, you are a practical director.

but beware

You need to be cautious about your frantic schedule. You can get so carried away with thoughts of supporting others that you can push yourself too far, both emotionally and physically. Excessive responsibilities will eventually destroy your passion and make you enraged. When you become burned out, you can become lazy and decadent. Allow yourself to relax. This will restore your energy and help you bounce back with a renewed, dedicated spirit.

red, green and brown

relationship tips

TO UNDERSTAND YOUR ENERGY IN A RELATIONSHIP, YOU FIRST NEED TO SELECT ANOTHER COLOR. Do you prefer yellow, blue, orange, or purple?

If you prefer yellow, you're a yellow-green; blue, a blue-green; purple, a red-purple; and orange, a red-orange.

NOW YOU NEED TO SELECT ANOTHER ACHROMATIC COLOR. Do you prefer black or white?

If you prefer black, add this new color to what you chose above to become a yellow-green-black, blue-green-black, red-orange-black, or a red-purple-black. If you prefer white, you become a yellow-green-white, blue-green-white, red-orange-white, or a red-purple-white. Now, turn to your new energy type found in this chapter and read how you are in your relationships.

work tips

Appreciate the power you have and stay on the lookout for what you and those around you need to be successful. You must feel that what you do somehow provides supportive structures or tools for others. Hands-on jobs in the medical field like a nurse or doctor, or in the human resources field like teaching or managing, will help you to better understand yourself.

things will be just fine if

...you put aside your concerns about life and just appreciate your accomplishments. Your new self-awareness will strengthen your belief in yourself. You will see how valuable you are to the world.

red, green and brown

THE ENTERTAINERS

discover yourself

By paying close attention to everyone's emotions, you better understand yourself and others. Your exciting, concerned energy compels people to express themselves. When you hear how others feel, you clearly see their kindness, love, pain, and fear. Your empathy makes them feel important. You captivate them by giving them all your attention. Isn't this the ultimate entertainer?

You help people pull their lives together. You are easily spotted at a party. You're the one to whom someone is always pouring their heart out. You love to discuss matters of the heart. This fuels your own desires.

dive in

Use your inexhaustible energy supply to make life an adventure for everyone. Show others how to start things over despite obstacles. Even when things are truly bad, you are able to regenerate and spice things up. Teach others not to be afraid to start something new or reinvent themselves. Tell them about your many experiences. When you're in charge and feeling good about your future, you are an inspiration to everyone.

but beware

Outside interference can make it difficult to complete your thorough thought process. This can destroy your ability to prioritize. Do not let others' opinions make you feel less powerful. They just don't have your ability to access all the issues. Request the autonomy and time to finish your projects and investigations.

relationship tips

You are sexy and seductive. You get what you want. But when love comes to an end, you know it and move on. You don't look back.

IF YOU CHOOSE YELLOW AS YOUR LEAST FAVORITE PRIMARY, you are focused on your love life. Problems occur when you get carried away with supporting the other person and they do not appreciate or respect you. Then there's hell to pay. Taking you for granted is a big mistake. You can hold a grudge. But staying angry wastes your valuable time and turns other people off. Find your happiness elsewhere.

IF YOU CHOOSE BLUE AS YOUR LEAST FAVORITE PRIMARY, you're aware of the many aspects that can cause a relationship to succeed or fail. Your ability to judge people accurately after first meeting them impresses others and is your great talent. However, you can get in trouble if you become distracted by too many thoughts and too much information.

work tips

You function best in a work environment where you're in control of all the resources you need and can motivate others. You have the power to calm those around you by being quick with solutions, not issuing blame. You think of ways to get things done behind the scenes.

You understand the importance of listening to other employees' concerns. You are a great team builder. Jobs in nursing, recruiting, politics, religion, or entertainment will make you feel important. You might even consider being a convention or event planner, an administrative assistant, or running a business where you can define all the terms.

things will be just fine if

...you put away your excessive thoughts about people and situations. You will regain a clear understanding of your feelings. When your heart leads, there's no stopping you.

THE FORECASTERS

discover yourself

You break everything down to its simplest form. Then you critique past events in order to see the future. Others are amazed at your predictions. You are a soothsayer. With your precautionary warnings, you make sure everything is considered. Others mistake your ability to interpret the facts as intuitive thinking.

dive in

You use common sense to its highest degree. Your insight creates new opportunities. You make sure that your message is heard and tell everyone the consequences they will suffer if they do not address their unrealistic expectations. Your respect for facts keeps you and others well grounded.

As long as you are not too close to a situation or a person, you are almost always right. You have the power to show people where they need to be spending their time and energy.

but beware

Your critical skills can limit your future, destroy your best ideas, opportunities, or passions. Too much analysis of everything that is going on can make you scattered. You can become extreme with relationships and endeavors.

So be direct with yourself. It will give you faith and courage to maintain a stronger focus on your objectives. You will be better able to manage the direction of your future.

red, purple and white

relationship tips

Your appearance and the way you dress are very together. Others will wonder where the chaos hides in you. You are wary of others until you really get to know them. The unknown arouses you. It may be frightening, but that's where the fun is. The downside is that the person you're with might not be trustworthy.

IF YOU CHOOSE YELLOW AS YOUR LEAST FAVORITE PRIMARY COLOR, you have an accurate idea of how to get the exact type of relationship you want. You can also assist others by sharing your relationship knowledge. When you do not give yourself the time to have a relationship, you can suddenly find yourself involved with exactly the one you were avoiding.

IF YOU CHOOSE BLUE AS YOUR LEAST FAVORITE PRIMARY COLOR, you see each item that will or will not work when you first meet someone. In your relationships, you can appear at times to be a bit dizzy. In reality, you are just trying to keep things fun and casual. This is mainly about your fear of commitment. Sometimes you are so worried about repeating past mistakes that you look for faults in people, and no one measures up to your standards.

work tips

You have the ability to get the job done right the first time. You are at your best when you are giving directions to the people in power. Expending a great deal of energy on each activity ensures your success.

You understand all the items that are needed to complete each task. This allows you to cut out unnecessary steps and not waste time. You will enjoy working with data, making predictions about the future, or analyzing exactly what is real or applicable to each situation.

things will be just fine if

...you stop bombarding yourself with information about everyone and everything around you. You will regain yourself.

red, purple and white

THE GENERATORS

discover yourself

Your concerned awareness gets attention wherever you go. Others see you as a curious character who needs to know about everything. You constantly attract opportunities. New people and situations stimulate you. You have the power to spice up others' lives. They boost your spirit and give you new perspectives that help you learn and grow.

dive in

Look around. See what looks good, then duplicate it for yourself. Make practical decisions on behalf of other people. Use your natural talents to define what they can do, even when they're drifting and clueless. Show people how to come to grips with the world around them. You'll be able to create bold new solutions.

but beware

Your great schemes and desires can cloud your judgment and keep you from accomplishing what is really needed. One moment you must have something, the next moment you are unsure. Are you making situations or relationships too exciting? When you feel too intense, slow down and rethink things so that you don't end up spinning your wheels.

relationship tips

TO UNDERSTAND YOUR ENERGY IN A RELATIONSHIP, YOU NEED TO SELECT ANOTHER ACHROMATIC COLOR. Do you prefer black or white?

If you prefer black, you're a red-purple-black. If you prefer white, you're a red-purple-white. Now, read the relationship tips in red-purple-black or red-purple-white found in this chapter to see how you are in your relationships.

work tips

Focus on careers where you can analyze your environment, see what looks promising, and then pursue it. It's easy for you to define yourself by what you do. You're a natural at jobs where you can generate enthusiasm for a product or design a better way of doing something. You can use talents and resources beyond what is normally viewed as their ultimate purpose.

things will be just fine if

...you know what you want before you expend your energy to acquire it.

red, purple and brown

THE CONSULTANTS

discover yourself

The journey to discover your inner self has you reminiscing over your past experiences. You are not afraid to contemplate what did not work and to seek new answers. Evaluating the past helps you better understand what will be of value to you in the future. Those who know you, trust you. They find you endearing.

dive in

You're the one people expect to get the ball rolling. This is your knack, so use it fully. Enjoy other people's appreciation, but don't think anyone else will be able to do for you what you've done for them. Reciprocation isn't what you're really looking for. Being in control, getting things done—this is satisfaction enough. So look for situations where you can lend a hand.

but beware

Avoid sentimentality and don't concentrate too much on the past. When you examine your emotions over and over, it is difficult for you to be objective. You lose sight of what you need or forget those who care most about you. Without a strong sense of devotion, you'll soon find yourself spiritually bankrupt. Let other people chase after their fantasies. You need to take care of your own business.

Give yourself the space to reappraise what you have now. Go for long walks or take an extended vacation by yourself. Distance will give you a new perspective. Once you get too close to something, it's hard for you to prioritize what or who is contributing to your growth.

relationship tips

When you know what you want, you aggressively go for it. Friends will see you as personable yet guarded. You are just afraid of being hurt.

IF YOU CHOOSE YELLOW AS YOUR LEAST FAVORITE PRIMARY COLOR, you are devoted. Problems occur when you get carried away with supporting other people. You lose your ability to know what is best for you. Your relationships can suffer. When you are upset, you seem to disappear. Are you questioning whether those you care about also care about you?

IF YOU CHOOSE BLUE AS YOUR LEAST FAVORITE PRIMARY COLOR, you find change particularly painful. You're afraid to commit to someone new or change the way you feel. You prefer to stick with the familiar, even though you know things aren't working. Confront these feelings and a genuine peace will follow.

work tips

Your loyalty and commitment create a powerful bond with people and form your key to success. Your sharp eye can see what's working; nothing can escape your penetrating gaze. You're a perfectionist. Who you work for means everything to you. You need to feel needed. You sacrifice your personal demands for the good of the company.

Jobs in which others can benefit from your support, such as medicine, childcare, or selling a product or service, are best for you.

things will be just fine if

...you let things happen spontaneously. This will create more magic in your life. Don't worry about losing control. Your life will become more about the present instead of a repeat of your past.

red, orange and black

THE RESOURCE DIRECTORS

discover yourself

You're all about setting priorities and maximizing the benefits you can receive from the things in your life. You may appear direct and focused on the issues at hand, but you're also deeply interested in the underlying dynamics of different relationships. You motivate people to take a closer look at their lives.

dive in

You realize that success lies in the details. You know how to take a good idea and make it into a great one. But your strength goes even further than that. Aim big. Create new options and better ways of using what you already have. Use your power of connecting resources to expand little ponds into big ones.

but beware

You play games with your feelings—often denying them. But feelings can't be turned into facts and vice versa. Make sure that what you have treasured in the past is not left behind. Don't become confused by new opportunities. New doesn't always mean better. Focus, or your heart will become empty.

relationship tips

You're a vivacious lover. Meeting new people is a turn on. But don't become a victim of excesses. In the end, your great need for intimacy will determine your happiness.

IF YOU CHOOSE YELLOW AS YOUR LEAST FAVORITE PRIMARY COLOR, you are on a journey to better understand how you feel. You are forever creating situations that seem to excite your emotions. Aren't you just creating drama to lose yourself? Don't lose sight of your own happiness. Slow down and others will see the genuine, lovable you.

IF YOU CHOOSE BLUE AS YOUR LEAST FAVORITE PRIMARY COLOR, you have a great need to be dedicated to someone. You can hide these feelings from others and sometimes even yourself. Are you avoiding your heart? Accept that emotions aren't dictated by logic. They'll always disrupt your life. And that's a good thing. Make a commitment to show your feelings. Others will see you as a teddy bear.

work tips

Choose work environments that allow you some freedom. This latitude will increase your focus and productivity and allow those in charge to recognize exactly what you can accomplish. Their appreciation will build your self-confidence. You'll be able to regenerate and become more powerful.

Show others better ways of using things. A few jobs you might be good at are career counseling, childcare worker, patent attorney, or computer technician.

things will be just fine if

...you allow others to see your emotional side. They'll be able to appreciate fully all the concerns you have and give you the attention that you need.

red, orange and white

THE INSPECTORS

discover yourself

You are very objective. Without any hesitation, you know exactly what needs to be done and you know from whom to request help. Like Sherlock Holmes, you are consistently discovering clues. You energize people by improving their lives.

Your dedication to others keeps you moving forward, especially when you're defending the underdog. When you fight for their causes, you are also working for your right to be appreciated. After all, every person has the right to be respected for what they do.

dive in

Take advantage of your directness. It eliminates nonsense and misconceptions. You are more concerned about what's going on than about people's interpretations. This is what makes you such a great inspector. Nothing can escape your sharp gaze.

Your concerns have healing power. You give of yourself, expecting nothing back other than honest appreciation. Express yourself by helping others with physical assistance or emotional reassurance. In doing this, you'll strengthen your own spirit.

but beware

You can become overly concerned with being needed. You are sometimes so worried about situations going wrong that you don't appreciate what's going right. At times, your supportiveness can overshadow the people you care about the most or hinder the completion of a task that is vital to your success. Slow down and contemplate the possibilities in your future. You will pick up speed later at an even more exciting pace.

relationship tips

TO UNDERSTAND YOUR ENERGY IN A RELATIONSHIP, YOU NEED TO SELECT ANOTHER ACHROMATIC COLOR. Do you prefer black or white?

If you prefer black, you're a red-orange-black; white, you're a red-orange-white. Now, read the relationship tips in red-orange-black or red-orange-white found in this chapter to see how you are in your relationships.

work tips

Use your awareness to fix problems. Your natural talent to fit things together will let you know instantly what will and will not be a success. When working with people, you know what they want to do.

Consider jobs that let you do things by yourself. Creating workable environments will give you great joy and make you feel important. Concentrate on showing your caring side. Do not allow your defensiveness to cloud your judgment.

things will be just fine if

...you free your mind from obligations. Goodness knows you have a lot of them! You'll obtain a clearer understanding of your needs without being influenced by others.

red, orange and brown

10 chapter

TAKING ON THE WORLD

Lime green, teal, indigo, magenta, red-orange, and gold are in the intermediate category. They represent how you approach the world. These energized hues spark you to act or react. They give you different perspectives that you need to direct your life. Get ready to view the ups and downs of your day! Select your intermediate colors from page 23.

IN THIS CHAPTER

YOUR TWO FAVORITE INTERMEDIATE COLORS indicate how you approach getting something. In an up moment, your selections reveal how you achieve success. You will read how the confident you attacks the world. Dwell on this apparent you and success will be yours.

YOUR TWO LEAST FAVORITE INTERMEDIATE COLORS show the perspectives you tend to forget. In a down moment, they disclose what you need to do yet never considered.

INTERMEDIATE COLORS INITIATE

The intermediate colors show how you make requests. Lime green, indigo, and red-orange push forward to inform you of what is needed. Magenta, teal, and gold lean back to create a space for you to see what is required. Both styles can be equally aggressive. As you read this chapter, look around you. Have fun watching others act out these visible characteristics.

LIME GREEN NOTES

> "It takes a very unusual mind to undertake the analysis of the obvious."
>
> ALFRED NORTH WHITEHEAD

lime green

in the beginning

You are incessantly contemplating what is missing in your life. You think about how it would feel to have certain things. Your strong sense of logic and no-nonsense style help people get to the heart of the matter. Even if they don't ask for help, eventually you will tell others what they need to do. Sometimes it seems so obvious, you can't help but blurt it out. You'll say exactly what other people are most afraid to hear. You recognize the consequences of avoiding essential needs.

you in action

Use your logic to establish the questions that need to be asked. Knowing the pertinent questions is as important as knowing the answers. Be the inventive person that you were meant to be. Don't let a misstep stop you from being a winner. Guide yourself, your projects, and those on your team to new methods or better ways of doing things.

key words
LOGICAL
SELF-INVESTIGATIVE

initiates
RATIONAL WAYS OF DOING THINGS

concerns
WHAT ELSE DO I NEED?

lime green

your highs

Your steady consideration of what you want allows you to exert logical control over what you start. You're seeking more change and adventure in life. Once you begin something, you don't quit. You grasp all the details needed for you to achieve your vision. This talent gives you an advantage in conversations and relationships. Others see you as a fast-thinking self-starter.

and lows

You become extremely introverted and get lost in your thoughts. When others fail to see what you've come to understand, you feel that you don't fit in. Sometimes you become consumed with your thoughts about what other people really need. Don't be so full of yourself. Others' needs are not going to be the same as yours. Go back to the period before your intense involvement or relationship began. Why did you start it in the first place? Then, clearly communicate your thoughts. Others will be better able to be on your team.

the seductive you

At first, you are a tough cookie, a hard person to get close to. Once you have accepted an individual, however, you get emotional about them. You become dedicated. When you are just starting a relationship, your self-awareness can be seen as sexy. When you walk into a room, everyone knows it.

your healing force

Your inward focus motivates others to contemplate what they really need.

YOU HAVE BAD TIMING

You tend to avoid looking inside of yourself to view what is missing in your life. Your refusal to be introspective can lead to frustration. You deny your needs for so long that eventually you just explode.

The good news is that you can find yourself in the middle of all kinds of adventures. The bad news is that the adventures don't meet your needs; they're simply what was available to you.

Initially you can avoid meeting "Mr. or Ms. Right," or confronting what you need in your present relationship. Then all of a sudden, you quickly meet someone or become overwhelmed about what is missing in your current relationship. This erratic behavior makes it difficult for you to know if what you have is what you want. It can send out confusing signals to your suitors or relationships.

When you find yourself repeatedly avoiding something you want, regard it as a warning sign. You need to take the time to ponder your repressed thoughts. Only then will you recognize the rewards and consequences of letting something or someone new into your life. Bad timing can waste a lot of your energy.

lime green LEAST FAVORITE

MAGENTA NOTES

> "Still round the corner
> there may wait, a new
> road, or secret gate."
>
> J.R.R. TOLKIEN

in the beginning

You surround yourself with friends who challenge you to grow. Your mind is seldom at rest. You are searching for inspiration and a sense of magic in your relationships and undertakings. The world is your oyster and you know how to get the most out of it for yourself and others. You have a genuine desire to bring about positive change.

you in action

Use your enthusiasm to regenerate yourself and those around you. Getting excited about what you already enjoy releases unlimited passion. Opportunities will seem just to appear. Teach your co-workers and loved ones to window shop—to concentrate on looking and not buying into a person or situation. They will see new avenues that will create more results with less effort.

key words
ENTHUSIASTIC
SOCIALLY INVESTIGATIVE

initiates
ATTRACTING NEW
PEOPLE AND
SITUATIONS

concerns
WHERE OR WITH WHOM
CAN I BECOME
INSPIRED?

your highs

You regenerate people. You have the power to spark new possibilities. Your need to believe in people helps them to believe in themselves. What they have longed to do becomes something they can do. You help others to see what will work for them.

and lows

When you don't prioritize, you start new things instead of finishing what you need to do. Many of your ideas may have been brilliant, if only they'd been realized. Here lies your frustration. To cope with this, you need to seek help to complete your tasks. After all, you didn't really want to finish all those projects you started, anyway. Contemplate your feelings. Realize that you don't need to take on new projects to keep from becoming bored. Completing things can be very exciting and rewarding. If you're able to say no to starting something new, that's half the battle.

the seductive you

Sometimes you are surprised at all the people you attract in life. You're like a magnet. Your body language entices others and then you're off together on an adventure.

You can't help but start something new in your relationships. You bring a certain sense of openness and curiosity to social situations. Your enthusiasm makes each day an event.

your healing force

Your curiosity opens others to see the opportunities in the world around them.

YOU ARE SUSPICIOUS

You need to feel inspired, but it is difficult for you. You're suspicious of new things and worry about taking on responsibility. If you start something, you feel that you will have to commit to finishing it.

You attract others who are inspired by their environment. Their enthusiasm opens your life. They force you to reveal your dreams to yourself. Recognize that you are going to start new things or you will lose control. New situations will just seem to occur.

When your energy is down, pay attention to your body language. If you are not looking forward to doing something or being with someone, it would be best for everyone, including you, to stay home.

Relax. Risk experiencing new things. Surround yourself with people who inspire you. Trust others to help you complete things. You will find yourself having a lot more fun. New adventures will suddenly appear.

in

you

magenta LEAST FAVORITE

teal

your highs

Sometimes you get up in the morning and feel like the most important person in the world. You feel you have the capabilities to accomplish whatever you want. You see your dreams within your grasp. Your past achievements become personal victories that make you proud.

and lows

Other times you feel as if you are not important at all, that you are pleasing others, not yourself. This can make it difficult for you to be creative. Stop being so concerned with what others think. Be honest with yourself. Muster the courage to speak up even when others do not want to listen. You will gain trust and respect from your peers. They will see you as more authentic.

the seductive you

You are very endearing. Sensitivity to other people's needs helps you to start new relationships. You try to become what the other person is looking for. You boost their confidence. This makes you very attractive.

Yet, your concerns about what others think can keep you from being completely honest. In your desire to be accepted, you sometimes say what people want to hear, instead of how you feel. Later on, they're in for a shock when your actions don't reflect your words. Being forthcoming about your own needs will go a long way toward making others feel comfortable.

your healing force

Your belief in others' dreams makes them believe in themselves.

YOU ARE SKEPTICAL

You work very, very hard because you have a deep need to show you are competent. You may tell yourself that you don't care about what others think, but this is just a defensive ploy.

When you voice or feel your skepticism, that's when you get into trouble and you later regret what you said or the impression you have conveyed. Even though you might have been right, was there anything gained by being negative?

Everyone knows where they stand with you. Many times this makes those close to you feel more comfortable. Others might hear, sometimes for the first time, how they are perceived. Your outspoken or skeptical nature can make it difficult to get close to you. Give the other person the opportunity to say what they really believe to be true, before you even think about your opinion.

Encourage others to seek their dream even when you don't believe in it. Remember, their dreams are about them, not you. Appreciate their positive energy. You'll become more optimistic about your own wishes.

RED-ORANGE NOTES

> "There is a road from the eye
> to the heart that does not
> go through the intellect."
>
> G.K. CHESTERTON

red-orange

in the beginning

You value the individual's right to a sense of dignity. By immersing yourself in life you are able to see what clicks and what does not. Your ability to commit yourself to a person makes them trust you. You appreciate the beauty of a person by making the time to be with them.

you in action

Use your sharp eye to monitor what is actually occurring around you. Set limits and establish standards that insure each person's honor and respect. Allow your unselfish devotion to make each individual feel important and you will become stronger. Others will feel your strength and gain the willpower to celebrate each person for what they do, not what they say or even think. Go ahead. Make the world around you more authentic.

key words
PERSONAL WORTH
SELF-RESPECT

initiates
RESPECT FOR THE
INDIVIDUAL

concerns
AM I RESPECTED?

red-orange

your highs

When you let your spirit flourish and show your sensitivity, your personal growth soars. You're able to appreciate what you have earned through your diligent efforts and make equitable comparisons in your situations and relationships. You make things work, even if all the ingredients for a solution aren't there.

By making aggressive suggestions on how to improve the lives of others, you exhibit your greatest attribute—true warmth in personal relationships. You appreciate each person for who they are.

and lows

In situations where you do not feel important, you can become overly sensitive and take things too personally. Your insecurity is obvious. You become defensive and critical. You make other people feel that you don't respect or appreciate them. If someone cuts in front of you in line, cheats, or lies, you become enraged and take it as a personal slight. Compassion is more appropriate than anger. People have their own problems and baggage to handle.

the seductive you

You are a loyal lover. This is very vital to your continued existence. When things aren't working, you know it. You forcefully try to ensure the trust and respect you deserve. You need an environment where you can be respected for your true self. You are happiest when you have a few good friends and a partner who idolizes you.

You love one-on-one relationships and pets because you need to experience unconditional love. When you talk to the people you care about, you often touch them with your hands. Touch allows you to trust. Others can misunderstand your affections as sexual aggressiveness.

your healing force

Your need to be respected encourages others to respect themselves.

YOU FORGET YOURSELF

You immerse yourself in being there for those you care about. You may accomplish your goal, but in the end you are no closer to understanding what makes you happy. Do you sometimes wonder where you stop and others begin?

Touch is a very personal thing with you. You are either aggressively lovable or avoid being touched. You have an emotional need to be touched, held, and appreciated for the beauty inside of you.

Others can see your request for affection as being sexually seductive or appearing to need attention. Express your vulnerability to those who care about you. You might be surprised, finding a lot more love than criticism.

Be more authentic to yourself. Pay more attention to who you are, not who you think you need to be. Feelings of being unloved will go away and you will be able to express your true warmth. Otherwise you'll lose out and feel like a victim.

red-orange LEAST FAVORITE

INDIGO NOTES

> "The world stands aside to let anyone pass who knows where they are going."
>
> DAVID STARR JORDON

indigo

in the beginning

You are focused on improving the future. Figuring out how to make your ideas a reality turns you on. Seeing things through to completion is the ultimate high. It gives you self-confidence.

When you're focused on creating an idea, you have the capacity to be the central, dramatic figure, which people can gather around. This directness makes you a natural leader. When you're in top form, no one questions your authority.

you in action

Use your futuristic thinking to create orchestrated plans. Put your doubts aside. Charge ahead with your thoughts. Discuss your idea with those around you. Revamp your original thought into a workable plan based on a consensus of exactly what is needed. Then jump right in, constantly considering if there is a better way, or even if you need assistance from someone else. Your unwavering focus will radiate self-confidence and eventually success.

key words
CONCEPTUAL
SELF-CONFIDENT

initiates
BEGINNINGS OF
CONSTRUCTIVE
THOUGHTS

concerns
CAN I CREATE A
WORKABLE PLAN?

your highs

Sometimes you have so much self-confidence you feel you can save the world. You love initiating new ideas, and safeguard their success by considering everything that can possibly go wrong. You assume that you can make things work. You are on a fast track to success. Others believe in you.

and lows

When your energy is down, even making toast becomes an act of courage. You have no self-confidence and feel scattered. During these low periods, you need a lot of attention. When people believe in you, you begin to believe in yourself. Many times friends help you realize that your feelings of disappointment are from having unrealistic expectations.

the seductive you

Your commanding, dramatic approach to things makes you appear very romantic. At times, however, you can be in love with the idea of love. This can make you see someone the way you want them to be, not the way they are. Initially, your dream person will meet all your expectations, but once you are romantically involved, you will see them as they really are, warts and all.

You have a tendency to be self-involved. This makes those who care about you feel unimportant. Connect with others and keep your expectations realistic.

your healing force

Your deep need to plan your life inspires others to invest more in themselves.

YOU PROCRASTINATE

You need to believe in your ability to plan your future. But to do so, you need a deeper level of commitment. If you just go through the motions and try to keep up appearances, you will never achieve your goals. You will not be able to combine your resources and talents effectively.

At first you will have a powerful, emotional connection with your "dream person." You see only the things you like and avoid looking at who they really are. You become completely immersed in the other person's plan. This can place you in a lot of situations that only appear fun. Avoid romantic disappointments by not being so spontaneous.

Recognize that it's easier to start new things when you can visualize what you want. Conduct an investigation. Piece together a plan for your future. Say exactly what you're going to do. You will become more focused on success and worry less about failure.

indigo LEAST FAVORITE

GOLD NOTES

> "In playing, we discover
> the essence of
> who we are."
>
> ANONYMOUS

in the beginning

Life is a game to be played. You demand a stimulating environment and the time to enjoy it. Meeting new people, discovering what your friends are thinking, and studying your surroundings are ways you gather information. With a probing curiosity, you uncover what you want and how to get it. Ideas come together to create new possibilities.

you in action

Use your foresight to see the value in each and every resource. Playfully examine each thing around you. Let your mind be free to associate the usability of each resource or others' talents. Make sure that you pause to communicate how you made or connected things together into workable situations. Your fast-thinking mind and uncanny ability to use resources can easily be overlooked. Document how you created exciting new things from nothing, and expect admiration.

key words
RESOURCEFUL
PLAYFUL

initiates
RELEASE OF
UNDESIRABLE
THOUGHTS

concerns
WHAT AM I
ENJOYING?

your highs

Downtime gives you the power to eliminate distractions and to rediscover what you enjoy. Methodically, you gather information. You see truths impartially and encourage others to talk about what they enjoy. Experiencing their passions mentally stimulates you. You can make people get really excited about doing something they generally would not do.

and lows

Overemphasis on fun distracts you from achieving more meaningful relationships. Making too many plans can be a way of avoiding emotional issues. You're so busy looking for the next thrill that you often forget to appreciate what you already have.

the seductive you

You see dating and courtship as an adventure. You experience different things and meet new people with an explosive spurt of energy. That's how you discover what's important to you in a relationship. But if you are not careful, your curiosity can get you into situations that you will later regret. Follow your natural inclination to get to know a person before getting too serious.

your healing force

Your excitement about the fun you've planned stirs passionate desire in others to do something new.

YOU FORGET WHAT'S FUN

You keep very busy. You follow a rigorous schedule to avoid thinking about what is not working in your life. This rugged pace runs down your battery and makes it difficult for you to know what you really want to do. Others can even see you as rigid.

Like a magnet, you attract others who are full of passion. In seeking to learn what you will enjoy, you listen to what others enjoy. Their interesting stories or the passion in their voice gets you excited. Their fun suggestions allow you to enjoy a day without your agendas.

Avoid asking serious questions. Instead, consider exaggerating your dilemma until you laugh. You will gain the objectivity to see beyond the many things that you must do. Others will see you as less controlling and more fun.

Take a day off to relax and be free from responsibilities. Go play! Try not to watch television, read, or even answer the phone. At first, you will feel uncomfortable. Later, however, you will gain an inner awareness that will eliminate undesirable thoughts and incidentals from your life.

COLOR COMMENTARY

Are you more thoughtful or action-oriented?

Rank the six intermediate category colors below in order of most to least favorite (1=most, 6=least).

Row #1   Magenta _____   Teal _____   Gold _____
Row #2   Lime Green _____   Red-orange _____Indigo _____

Now, consider only your top three favorites. How many are in Row #1? Row #2?

Row #1 _____   (Magenta, Teal, Gold)
Row #2 _____   (Lime Green, Red-orange, Indigo)

If you selected two of your top three favorites from…

Row #1, you are mostly thoughtful.
Row #2, you are mostly action-oriented.

Read the description of thoughtful and action-oriented on the next page.

thoughtful

You are foremost concerned with your thoughts. First you consider how the other person or a situation affects you. Your considerations attract others like a giant magnet. Simply stated, when you think about someone, they think about you. You are inspiring. This is especially true if you selected all of your top three favorites from Row #1.

Sometimes it is best for you to just do it. You will never know what you want until you try it.

action-oriented

You prefer taking action rather than waiting for things to come. Your concern to do what you want attracts those who need change. Your constant motion forces others to move too. You motivate others to do for themselves. This is especially true if you selected all of your top three favorites from Row #2.

Sometimes it is best for you to let life come to you. Be more thoughtful about what you want before you act and your life will be richer.

laughing out loud

Extremes attract extremes. Wherever you are out of balance you attract people and situations that give or teach you exactly what you need to know. These lessons can be inspiring, life-altering, even horrifying.

Consider what you have learned from the most wonderful and also the most terrifying person or situation that you have encountered. Now applaud or laugh at yourself.

WHEN YOUR INTERMEDIATE COLORS CHANGE

Your intermediate colors change more than any of the other colors. When your goals change, they often change, too. Get really mad or really happy and you'll see an immediate change in your intermediate color preferences. For the most part, however, your favorite and least favorite colors remain constant.

HOW COLOR LANGUAGE EVOLVED

How each intermediate color was given language is described below.

lime green is self-investigation

Yellow, the search for a more realistic perspective, and green, nurturing, combine to make lime green. Together they generate the power to question what is missing in your life.

teal is believing in your future

Green, nurturing, and blue, future-based planning, combine to make teal. Together they generate the power to nurture and believe in your dreams.

indigo is creating a plan

Blue, future-based planning, and purple, seeing possibilities, combine to make indigo. Together they generate the power to plan an exciting future.

magenta is becoming inspired

Purple, seeing possibilities, and red, directing resources, combine to make magenta. Together they generate the power to be inspired and enthusiastically embrace the world around you.

red-orange is self-respect

Red, directing resources, and orange, dissecting out what is not working, combine to make red-orange. Together they generate the power to respect your individuality.

gold is regeneration of your soul

Orange, dissecting out what is not working, and yellow, the search for a realistic perspective, combine to make gold. Together they generate the power to play and discover the essence of your passions.

THE INTERMEDIATE IQ
ANSWER TRUE OF FALSE

lime green favorite intermediate color
1. Asks a lot of questions.   T or F

lime green least favorite intermediate color
2. Always accepts what he or she needs.   T or F

magenta favorite intermediate color
3. Loves finishing what he or she starts.   T or F

magenta least favorite intermediate color
4. Is difficult to inspire.   T or F

red-orange favorite intermediate color
5. Can become concerned with high society.   T or F

red-orange least favorite intermediate color
6. Is seeking unconditional love.   T or F

teal favorite intermediate color
7. Is a great listener.   T or F

teal least favorite intermediate color
8. Works harder and harder to recognize their   T or F
   accomplishments.

indigo favorite intermediate color
9. Appears very confident.   T or F

indigo least favorite intermediate color
10. Isn't concerned about planning the future.   T or F

gold favorite intermediate color
11. Is all work and no play.   T or F

gold least favorite intermediate color
12. Is very busy.   T or F

ANSWERS TO THE INTERMEDIATE QUIZ

lime green favorite intermediate color
1. T   They need to know all the facts.

lime green least favorite intermediate color
2. F   No, no, no, or is that yes, yes, yes?

magenta favorite intermediate color
3. F   New is more fun.

magenta least favorite intermediate color
4. T   Their suspicious nature can border on paranoia.

red-orange favorite intermediate color
5. F   A few good friends are more important than an expensive bottle of champagne.

red-orange least favorite intermediate color
6. T   They hide it really well.

teal favorite intermediate color
7. T   Communication comes naturally.

teal least favorite intermediate color
8. T   Even being President of the United States is not enough.

indigo favorite intermediate color
9. T   Much more than they really are.

indigo least favorite intermediate color
10. T   Least favorite indigos are terrified of it.

gold favorite intermediate color
11. F   When left alone, trouble is brewing.

gold least favorite intermediate color
12. T   Fun takes a lot of work.

HAPPINESS AND HEALING

Until now, you've learned only about the primary, secondary, achromatic, and intermediate colors. Now you will learn the meaning of an additional 45 colors, the color shades. Look on pages 26-29 for the full array of color shades. Relax and let these healing colors pick you.

IN THIS CHAPTER

THE COLOR SHADES WILL REVEAL THE INTERNAL MONOLOGUE YOU CARRY ON WITH YOURSELF—the concerns and desires you have but are hesitant to admit to yourself.

USE THE COLOR MEANINGS OF THESE SHADES AS A BACKDOOR APPROACH to understanding yourself. You will become happier and heal your past.

COLOR SHADES REVEAL YOUR NEEDS

These 45 endearing colors will disclose those thoughts that you consider, but then forget or reject. You will gain the knowledge to see below the tip of your self-made iceberg. Bring your suppressed needs to the surface, discard your concerns, dwell on your desires, and use these color meanings to better plan your life.

YOUR MENTAL NOTES

THE MENTAL YOU

IN SELECTING YOUR FAVORITE LIME GREEN, GREEN, TEAL, AND BLUE SHADES, you will discover your somewhat disclosed thoughts about your future. Your favorite mental color shades indicate how you are focusing on your goals, avoiding reactionary thoughts, and creating new ideas.

TURN BACK TO PAGE 26 AND SELECT
YOUR TWO FAVORITE MENTAL SHADES.

what you'll learn

Your brain waves are in a constant flux. They are searching for a definite direction, yet need the freedom to include new ideas. The mental shades indicate what you need to become mentally centered, envision a future, and maintain a steady concentration. Your mind needs silence to process information. Mental healing and happiness begins with serenity.

THE MENTAL SHADES
COMPLETE YOUR THOUGHTS

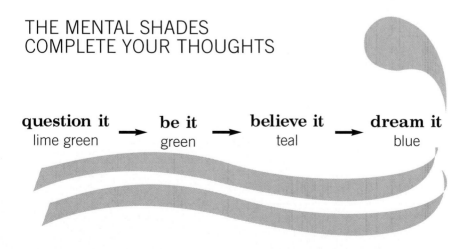

question it
lime green → **be it**
green → **believe it**
teal → **dream it**
blue

LIME GREEN SHADES

You are aggressively searching to better understand your needs. The lime green shades show how you are assessing what is missing in your life so you can solve your problems.

SPRING GREEN: lime green with white

You seek more freedom and inner peace. Too many commitments can be restrictive. You carefully consider the consequences before starting anything new. You want the freedom to know different environments, make new friends, and acquire a fresh perspective on the inner you.

Be careful. Your feelings more accurately reflect what you need than your logical thought processes do. Embrace your emotions or you will find yourself repeating the same dead-end patterns of behavior.

CAMEL: lime green with brown

You need to sample new pleasures and enjoy living in the moment. Things happen spontaneously. Only later do you reflect back on events and decide if you'd like to experience them again.

As long as you accept your behavior as healthy, things will be fine. It is normal to have physical wants.

PALM GREEN: lime green with black

When you're alone, you constantly question what is missing in your life. You want to know how to create a more passionate future. By investigating your feelings, you hope to identify what truly inspires you.

Don't become self-obsessed or overly concerned with what is missing in your life. Dwelling on things too long will rob you of any chance at happiness. People will see you as self-centered.

GREEN SHADES

You want to be nurtured and better supported. The green shades show where you are examining yourself and others to create stronger emotional bonds.

MINT GREEN: green with white

You wish to recognize who else can be truly important to you. Knowing you can always attract a safety net of caring friends and a stable job will calm many of your fears. You're constantly making supportive suggestions.

Be careful. Seeking new adventures and relationships can make those you care about feel unimportant. It can also make it difficult for them to appreciate the balance you bring to their life.

OLIVE: green with brown

You are seeking to be more grounded and secure. By sharing your concerns about others, you receive supportive, practical solutions that make your life work better. Others see you as very giving. You're really fun to be with.

Make sure that when you sample new things, you don't become distracted and lose your own values in the process.

EMERALD: green with black

You stay in touch with your feelings so that you can know deeper love. You look to your past for guidance. This gives you the power to create a natural sense of harmony in your relationships.

When you're upset, you can ignore good suggestions from friends. Concentrate on improving your future. Don't feel slighted by their comments. Most of the time they are trying to be helpful.

TEAL SHADES

You are examining how to accomplish your dreams. The teal shades show how you are believing in your wishes.

SEA GREEN: **teal with white**

You envision your future and see all the options needed to get there. This is your great power. You emphasize the positive, but keep dreams realistic. You give others the ability to believe in themselves. Their faith in you enhances your self-esteem.

You need the space to objectively view what is required to keep your dream alive. Recognize that feeling lonely is a self-imposed method of critiquing yourself.

OCEAN BLUE: **teal with brown**

You are looking for more practical methods to achieve your wishes. By redirecting your actions or communicating the same thing a different way, you are getting your point across. Right now you especially need others to validate your accomplishments.

Be careful. Don't you really want to know if what you are wishing is what you want? If you procrastinate, your concerns about what other people think can stop you from starting what you need.

FOREST GREEN: **teal with black**

You feel intensely about your dreams and what you've done in the past. Approval from others gives you the confidence to get things started. You are at your best when you are supporting other people's dreams.

Don't let your pride get in the way. Tell others what you are capable of accomplishing. Otherwise you'll become overly sensitive to their comments.

BLUE SHADES

You are continually rethinking your future. The blue shades show how you connect your goals to your passions.

SKY BLUE: **blue with white**

You see the world as it could be. Ever idealistic, your faith in your ideas and principles gives you the inner strength to believe more in yourself. Aren't you trying to live a life that you can be proud of?

Don't let your romantic notions create unrealistic expectations. Take the time to appreciate what you contribute to situations. You'll find this helps motivate you to achieve your goals.

EARTH: **blue with brown**

You are stable and have both feet on the ground. Because you know exactly what you want, you're able to offer practical advice to others. Seeing the end product is especially important to you. It keeps you motivated.

Watch out. You can become too wrapped up in what you are doing and fail to see other possibilities. Think more about tomorrow, or you might find yourself settling for less.

NAVY: **blue with black**

You visualize your future, and then you plan it. You categorize your thoughts. Knowing what your future holds gives you a sense of stability. It allows you to anticipate the outcome and get excited. Once you get going, it is hard to stop you.

Your future will never turn out the way you planned it. Don't try to force others or situations to meet your expectations. Take more risks. Your life will become more exciting and successful.

your mental requests

YOUR PHYSICAL NOTES

THE PHYSICAL YOU

IN SELECTING YOUR FAVORITE INDIGO, PURPLE, MAGENTA, AND RED SHADES, you will see how you are arranging the world around you to be more about what you want. Your favorite physical color shades reveal how you are making your life more pleasurable and successful.

TURN BACK TO PAGE 27 AND SELECT
YOUR TWO FAVORITE PHYSICAL SHADES.

what you'll learn

Your physical energy and emotions are in a constant flux. They are searching to balance dedication to others with the need to be yourself. Excessiveness of either can make you feel lost, selfish, or less important. The physical shades reveal how you search to become emotionally centered, maintain positive relationships, love, and allow others to love you. Physical healing and happiness starts with positive experiences.

THE PHYSICAL SHADES
EXPRESS ACTION

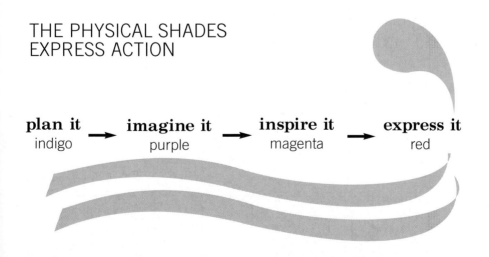

plan it → **imagine it** → **inspire it** → **express it**
indigo   purple   magenta   red

INDIGO SHADES

You are focused on creating new ideas to become more self-confident. The indigo shades show how you motivate yourself to plan your future.

PERIWINKLE: **indigo with white**

You live for new ideas. Believing in your ideas allows you to believe in yourself. You compulsively consider how to make your dreams come true. When you are focused, your optimistic approach gives you an air of self-confidence.

If you are feeling lost and unable to enjoy even positive changes, you are not being realistic. Give your mind a rest and you will regain the power to create a more workable plan.

SIENNA: **indigo with brown**

You are searching for practical solutions to accomplish your dreams. Your sharp awareness can direct exactly what needs to be done. You are a doer. The more things you undertake, the more self-confident you become.

Make sure that each action you've taken is part of a plan that will help you arrive at your goal. The best things in life, many times, are worth waiting for.

COBALT: **indigo with black**

You are determined to create your own ideas to develop self-confidence. You become self-absorbed to assess your capabilities. Your mind is constantly planning how to create something new. Others see you as confident.

Don't become consumed with self-doubt if the solution doesn't come quickly. Believe more in your ability to create. Your self-confidence will return.

PURPLE SHADES

You want to understand how powerful you can be in your current situations and relationships. The purple shades show how you are investigating your capabilities.

LAVENDER: **purple with white**

You enjoy creating passionate situations. You regularly look for new ways to reinvigorate your relationships. You can be quite risqué with those who are loyal to you. Experiencing a wider range of feelings gives you a healing approach to life.

Be aware that by emphasizing the new, you might be seen as failing to appreciate what is already making you happy.

GRAPE: **purple with brown**

Like a scientist, you examine things. Then you experiment with how to improve upon them. Your factual, no-nonsense approach makes you appear very bold. You express yourself as a knowledgeable person.

Be careful. You can waste a lot of your time and resources trying to prove a point, instead of taking care of what needs to be done.

DARK PURPLE: **purple with black**

You seek to understand your underlying motivations. By identifying the emotions behind specific actions, you hope to gauge your own potential. You have a tremendous ability to recognize hidden motivations.

Don't let past disappointments or current obsessions distract you from focusing on what's most important to you.

MAGENTA SHADES

You are surrounding yourself with stimulating people and situations. The magenta shades show where you need to be less skeptical and more enthusiastic.

ORCHID: **magenta with white**

You are constantly thinking about exciting things to do. Through your body language and appearance, you send out enticing messages, which you are not aware of. Regardless of your motivations, you are going to find new challenges.

Be careful. Don't let your need for stimulation cause you to attract extremes. You'll get more than you bargained for.

GARNET: **magenta with brown**

Life has to be fun, full of adventurous people. Even though you do not want to rock the boat, somehow you stir things up. Doesn't your curiosity encourage others to express what makes them passionate? You have the power to motivate those you care about to do what makes them happy.

Your adventurous thoughts and impulsive nature attract new people and situations. Be aware of who and what appears.

MULBERRY: **magenta with black**

By understanding the mysteries and depth of your environment, you hope to add dimension to your relationships. You enjoy hearing the passion in people's voices as they talk about past adventures. Their energy helps to inspire in you a new excitement about your present projects. You can attract some real characters.

Warning! Your need to experience passion can cause you to misjudge and overvalue things. Later, you can become disappointed and lose interest when they don't satisfy your needs. Sometimes you search all over the world and still find you're not happy.

RED SHADES

You need to be more aware of how you feel. The red shades show how you are expressing yourself in order to realize who you are.

PINK: **red with white**

Your genuine concern for others can make you appear angelic. You seek to convey your spirit by giving. It is your great strength. You have the power to heal those you care about.

Even though you give, expecting nothing in return, you must receive back unconditional love to continue on your journey in life. Tell others what you need. It will enable them to reciprocate your endearing love.

APPLE RED: **red with brown**

You have a need to explore physical sensations. Hugs heal you. Relationships bring out the best in you. Those who are close to you receive solutions. You have a talent for making things work.

People often judge you by your appearance or your accomplishments, not by the goodness of your heart. Spend a moment with each person you meet. Let them know how you feel, not just what you are thinking or doing.

CRANBERRY: **red with black**

In the past, you have felt that you did not have the freedom to be yourself. That is who you used to be. Now, you are determined to say who you are. When you speak, others feel that they know you. Your voice motivates them to be themselves.

Don't let your past feelings overpower you. Chances are you have already discarded what does not work in your life and have grown more than you realize.

YOUR SPIRITUAL NOTES

THE SPIRITUAL YOU

IN SELECTING YOUR FAVORITE RED-ORANGE, ORANGE, GOLD, AND YELLOW SHADES, you reveal your search to maintain a more steady awareness of everyone and everything around you. Your favorite spiritual shades disclose how you are attracting a life where you can be yourself.

TURN BACK TO PAGE 28 AND SELECT
YOUR TWO FAVORITE SPIRITUAL SHADES.

what you'll learn

Your spiritual energy is in a constant flux to understand yourself. Your spiritual shade selection highlights your quest to feel more alive. An excessive preoccupation with personal freedom or being overly concerned about others can make it difficult to know and honor yourself. Being spiritually centered gives you the capacity to grow, learn, and make your life an expression of your inner self. Spiritual healing and happiness starts with forgiveness.

THE SPIRITUAL SHADES
UNDERSTAND YOUR SOUL

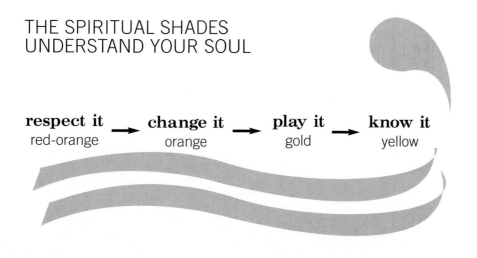

respect it → **change it** → **play it** → **know it**
red-orange — orange — gold — yellow

RED-ORANGE SHADES

You are demanding respect as an individual. The red-orange shades show how you seek to be appreciated and loved.

SALMON: **red-orange with white**

You explore the past to find value and meaning. Deep down, are you considering the purpose of your life and who will miss you when you're gone? Recognition of your accomplishments and the strength of your relationships will re-establish your principles and values. It will give you the passion to fight the good fight.

When you're upset, don't overintellectualize situations. True worth can only be felt in your heart or in the happiness of those who care about you.

WARM RED: **red-orange with brown**

You express yourself with great flair. Letting your natural personality come through and being of help to people make you feel good. Touch is of great importance to you.

Your constant concern for others fuels your ability to get things done. However, later you can become frustrated when you feel that people are just using you and don't care about your needs. Do not allow your disappointment in people to keep you from expressing your warm spirit.

RUBY: **red-orange with black**

You are concerned about what makes you special. You analyze your feelings to see what makes you different from others. Everyone knows your beliefs. By taking a stand, you become the stronger individual that you wish to be. You are better able to appreciate yourself and to heal your past wounds.

If you focus too much on your principles, you can unintentionally create distance in your relationships. Those you reject may see you as insensitive.

ORANGE SHADES

You want to understand what is and is not working in your life. The orange shades show what you are dwelling on to gain more realistic expectations.

APRICOT: **orange with white**

You are steadily examining your past actions and perspectives to create a more positive future. Asking questions about your feelings helps you to see how the loss of a friend, a lover, or even a job will impact your life. You have the power to create hope.

Don't let your thoughts about tomorrow or remorse about the past inhibit you from expressing your warm, lovable side.

CLAYPOT: **orange with brown**

You are at your best when you are supporting others. This lets you understand what you want. You become refreshed, able to appreciate all the things that you are doing. You do not expect anything in return except honest appreciation.

Your embrace has healing power, but be careful that your affections aren't misunderstood. Focus on helping those who truly appreciate you. Needing you is just not enough.

MAHOGANY: **orange with black**

You are working at getting to know your feelings. By constantly examining how you felt in the past, you see what is not of importance. At times, you can be torn between your own feelings and others' expectations.

Your preoccupation with the past and sentimental feelings can drain your energy. People lean on you more than they should. This can interfere with your ability to take care of your own business.

GOLD SHADES

You are searching for what gives you joy. The gold shades show how you are acquiring the freedom to eliminate undesirable thoughts to focus on your passions.

GOLDEN: **gold with white**

At present, you see many things that you want. Considering what would feel good is very healing to you. Are you asking yourself, "If I had a sunny, happy life, how would I feel? What would I be doing?" These thoughts illuminate you. They give new perspectives.

Be careful. You can overschedule or avoid planning fun activities. Be decisive. Say exactly what you want to do. Do not get distracted.

BRONZE: **gold with brown**

Right now, all you want to do is have some fun. You are seeking to rediscover your more playful spirit. By allowing yourself to do what you want to do, you create passion for yourself and others.

Establish a plan to create a more lasting happiness for yourself. Otherwise, you may become too absorbed in fleeting pleasures.

LEAF: **gold with black**

You are insisting on more opportunity to do what makes you happy. Now is the time to do what you want to do. At the root of your new perspective is a desire to be more passionate and truer to yourself.

You are about to enter a period of your life when you will feel better about yourself and what you do. Hold onto this new you. You will find unknown levels of energy. Others will see you as a burst of excitement.

YELLOW SHADES

You want to be more aware of your needs. The yellow shades show what you are gravitating toward to make you feel more alive.

PALE YELLOW: **yellow with white**

You are seeking to be more objective in your relationships and situations. Being less dependent allows you to understand what you and others need. With this natural grounding, your awareness creates hope and a promise of a brighter future.

However, your ability to foresee events makes you feel responsible for communicating impending problems. If you dwell on this negativity, you'll destroy your passions.

MUSTARD: **yellow with brown**

You are very concerned about how to make your surroundings and those you care about more comfortable. Like a scientist, you are realistically examining things. You clearly see how to make the physical world better.

Be careful. Don't neglect the important people in your life because others seem to need you more. Look again. Chances are those who really care about you need you just as much.

MOSS: **yellow with black**

You are forever seeking to be more realistic about what you need. One moment you accept the way things are, and the next moment you are uncertain if they are working. You have the power to see both the positive and negative about each person or situation.

Don't let your constant considerations distract you. You will become spellbound, caught up in your own concerns.

YOUR SILENT NOTES

THE SILENT YOU

IN SELECTING YOUR FAVORITE BLACK, BROWN, AND WHITE SHADES, you will learn what you are instinctively requesting to be more complete with yourself. Your favorite achromatic color shades reveal how you are rediscovering the inner you to create hope.

TURN BACK TO PAGE 29 AND SELECT
YOUR TWO FAVORITE SILENT SHADES.

what you'll learn

The silent shades indicate how your decision process is affecting your course in life. Use these messages to become more centered and better able to prioritize your thoughts and actions. Make your fate more about what you need than what the world is giving you. Prioritize people and situations that allow you to grow and learn.

THE SILENT SHADES CONNECT THE MENTAL, PHYSICAL, AND SPIRITUAL YOU

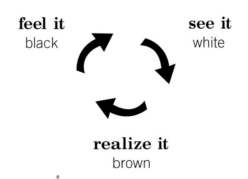

feel it
black

see it
white

realize it
brown

BLACK SHADES

You are seeking to define better what you need. The black shades show how you are confronting your concerns to become aware of what you truly value.

PEWTER: **mostly white with black**

You are always thinking of new ways to do things. At decision time, you seek new resources or different ways to make things work. Even if you are very determined to do something, when the chips are down you become open to change.

Under stress, you often lose track of your goals. You think too much. Stop endlessly assessing your future and a plan of action will become apparent.

GRAY: **black balanced with white**

You are cautious. You consider every option before you act. Under pressure, you keep your cool. Others appreciate this power. You make them feel good about themselves.

Be careful. You can become fixated on your thoughts. Just do it, even if it makes you feel uncomfortable. Your life will become less mental, more fun.

CHARCOAL: **mostly black with white**

You are disciplined and mentally focused. Knowing exactly what tomorrow will bring makes you feel secure. Your positive energy creates new things and allows others to feel good about themselves. You are like a cheerleader to your friends, readily pointing out how important they are.

When you're under pressure, however, you dwell on the past instead of dealing with the present. Be more objective and less sensitive. Not everything is about you.

BROWN SHADES

By living in the moment, you are seeking to be more aware of what you want. The brown shades show where you need to be more authentic to yourself.

DESERT: white with brown

You love to look around and see what is available. New is fun. Looking stimulates your desires. Considering something or someone new creates passion within you. It gives you the power to see easier ways of getting what you want.

When you're upset, however, you want everything. This makes it very difficult for you to define what you need. Dwell longer on what you want to do before you do it. Make sure it is what you need.

TAN: brown balanced with white

You have the vision to see what will give you the most pleasure in life. By evaluating what you want on a regular basis, you acquire the power of knowing who or what is best for you. You know when a person is excessive or is not comfortable with his or her desires.

Your defense mechanisms and routines can keep you from doing what you want to do. If you don't take a few more risks, you will stagnate.

BROWN-BLACK: mostly brown with black

You are a headstrong force who is demanding to get what you want. You are not indecisive. You have the power to plot your course. You are a go-getter.

Be careful. You can be obstinate. Constantly ask yourself, "Am I fulfilling my present needs or am I a slave to my past wants?" Otherwise, you will arrive at your destination feeling empty.

WHITE SHADES

You wish to pursue new options. The white shades show you how you are calculating what bodes well for your future.

ALMOND: **mostly white with yellow**

You are looking to balance your life by questioning who and what you really need. You need to experience life moment by moment and to have great spiritual closeness with someone in order to be healed.

Be careful. In your search, everything or everyone seems to match at the beginning. After a while, however, you are able to feel who or what is creating more passion in your life. Don't make comments about what you need to do until you are sure that you want it.

BEIGE: **mostly white with brown**

You are conducting a search to experience new desires. You want to feel more complete. Your hope is to control your expectations by desiring only the things you can get.

Currently, you are attracting many different types of people and things, not all of which are good for you. Initially you accept them. This can get you into jams. Don't be so wishy-washy. Say what you want to do.

TAUPE: **mostly white with brown and black**

You are investigating new options. One moment you are defining how you feel, the next you are viewing what else you could do. Planning new ways to create relationships, resources, and things gives you what you need.

Prioritizing what to do first can be a chore. Your hesitation about taking action can make you feel uninspired and bland. Remind yourself over and over again of what is important in your life. You'll gain the courage to take action.

12 chapter
COLOR SHOPPING GUIDE

Welcome to nature's way of using color tone to blend and create harmony. No longer do you have to fear an obnoxious color mismatch. Use this shopping guide to be daring. Add a polished finishing touch to what you already own or create new and exciting outfits and rooms.

IN THIS CHAPTER

CONCENTRATE ON HOW YOU FEEL as you view these exciting and harmonic color combinations.

CONSIDER THE POSSIBILITIES OF USING THESE 60 DIFFERENT COLORS in over 3,000 coordinating combinations.

KEEP YOUR OPTIONS OPEN. Chapter 13, "Color Coordinate You," and Chapter 14, "Color Your World," will show you innovative examples of how to make this guide work for you.

BECOME EMPOWERED
Using colors that stimulate your emotions will enhance your self-image and make your life more of a passionate adventure. Loosen up. Forget how you normally coordinate your wardrobe or decorate your surroundings.

Selecting the colors you prefer most will give you the confidence to believe more in yourself. Combine them with your least favorite colors and you will be amazed, after awhile, at your emotionally soothing attraction to them.

BECOME A COLOR EXPERT

Use this guide to become a skillful, sophisticated color expert. Before you become immersed in coordinating colors, follow these three easy steps.

step #1: evaluate your resources

View each item in your room, outfit, or design as a separate entity. Decide what you are going to keep and what you want to discard. Don't discount an outfit, room, or fabric until you have considered the possibilities. Be mostly concerned at this stage with how it fits you or your overall scheme, not the color itself. Later, you will experience how this system gives you the latitude to change colors that do not work into a rousing success.

step #2: match your existing colors

Look at your fabric, couch, hair, table, counter tops, cabinets, or current paint or print color next to the 60 colors on pages 242, 243, and 244. You will be able to get a correct match. Some colors will be in-between colors. Try matching these with both of the colors. One will work. Those that are a little darker or lighter will still match with a color of the same hue.

step #3: take the guide shopping

Take this book with you when you're buying clothes, furnishings, or creating new designs. Not only will you learn how to coordinate colors, you'll also be able to make empowering color statements to the world around you.

After you hit the stores, hold the shopping guide next to the couch, shirt, chair, pants, table, or skirt you are considering to establish an exact color hue match. Does it coordinate with a row, triadic, complement, or split complement? Now look around. How else can you spice up your outfits and room decor?

Embrace Hue You Are™

|d|e|w|e|y| color system™

the energizing spectrum row

| LIME GREEN COLUMN | GREEN COLUMN | TEAL COLUMN | BLUE COLUMN | INDIGO COLUMN | PURPLE COLUMN |

the enlightening white row

| SPRING GREEN | MINT GREEN | SEA GREEN | SKY BLUE | PERIWINKLE | LAVENDER |

the embracing brown row

| CAMEL | OLIVE | OCEAN BLUE | EARTH | SIENNA | GRAPE |

the empowering black row

| PALM GREEN | EMERALD | FOREST GREEN | NAVY | COBALT | DARK PURPLE |

the energizing spectrum row

MAGENTA
COLUMN

RED
COLUMN

RED-ORANGE
COLUMN

ORANGE
COLUMN

GOLD
COLUMN

YELLOW
COLUMN

the enlightening white row

ORCHID   PINK   SALMON   APRICOT   GOLDEN   PALE YELLOW

the embracing brown row

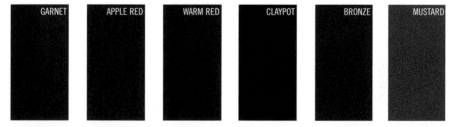

GARNET   APPLE RED   WARM RED   CLAYPOT   BRONZE   MUSTARD

the empowering black row

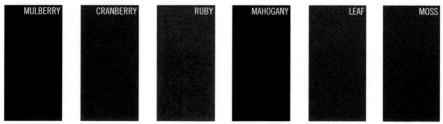

MULBERRY   CRANBERRY   RUBY   MAHOGANY   LEAF   MOSS

|d|e|w|e|y| color system ™

|d|e|w|e|y| color system ™

the energizing spectrum row

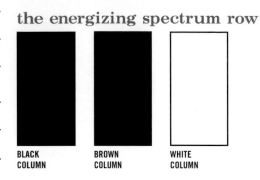

BLACK COLUMN **BROWN COLUMN** **WHITE COLUMN**

the enlightening white row

PEWTER DESERT ALMOND

the embracing brown row

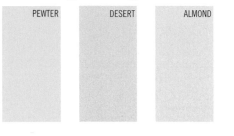

GRAY TAN BEIGE

the empowering black row

CHARCOAL BROWN-BLACK TAUPE

COLOR BASICS

Coordinate the colors on this page with their rows on pages 242 and 243 to enhance their color.

These color basics will tone down brilliant colors or your mood! You will learn more specific ways to make these seductive colors work for you in chapters 13 and 14.

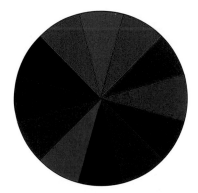

accomplish your goals
Combine the Yellow, Blue, and Red Rows

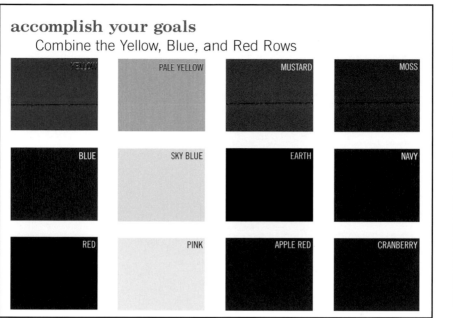

YELLOW | PALE YELLOW | MUSTARD | MOSS

BLUE | SKY BLUE | EARTH | NAVY

RED | PINK | APPLE RED | CRANBERRY

relate better to others
Combine the Green, Purple, and Orange Rows

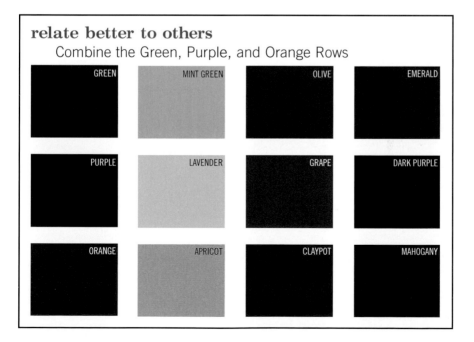

GREEN | MINT GREEN | OLIVE | EMERALD

PURPLE | LAVENDER | GRAPE | DARK PURPLE

ORANGE | APRICOT | CLAYPOT | MAHOGANY

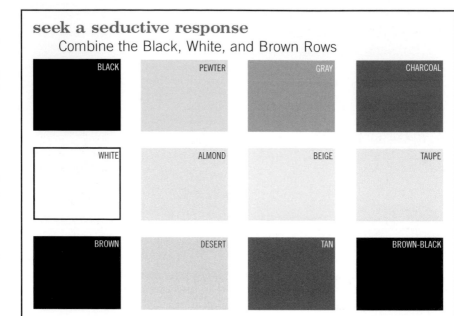

seek a seductive response
Combine the Black, White, and Brown Rows

BLACK	PEWTER	GRAY	CHARCOAL
WHITE	ALMOND	BEIGE	TAUPE
BROWN	DESERT	TAN	BROWN-BLACK

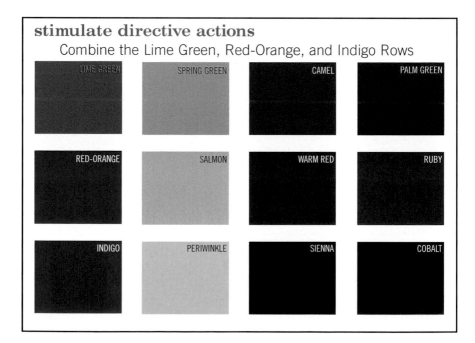

stimulate directive actions
Combine the Lime Green, Red-Orange, and Indigo Rows

LIME GREEN	SPRING GREEN	CAMEL	PALM GREEN
RED-ORANGE	SALMON	WARM RED	RUBY
INDIGO	PERIWINKLE	SIENNA	COBALT

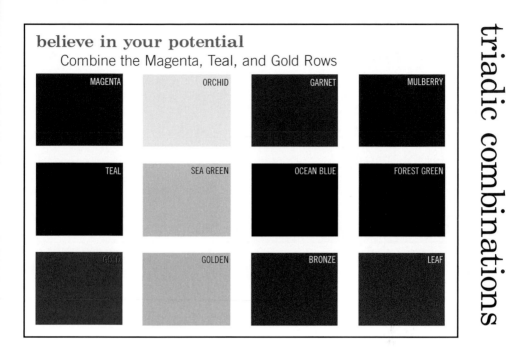

believe in your potential
Combine the Magenta, Teal, and Gold Rows

MAGENTA	ORCHID	GARNET	MULBERRY
TEAL	SEA GREEN	OCEAN BLUE	FOREST GREEN
GOLD	GOLDEN	BRONZE	LEAF

triadic combinations

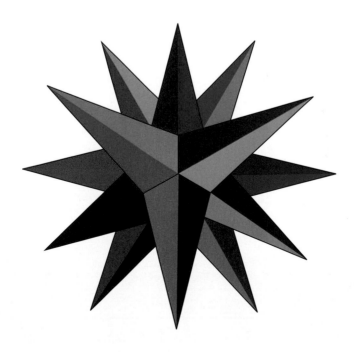

color complements

strengthen your spirit
Combine the Yellow and Purple Rows

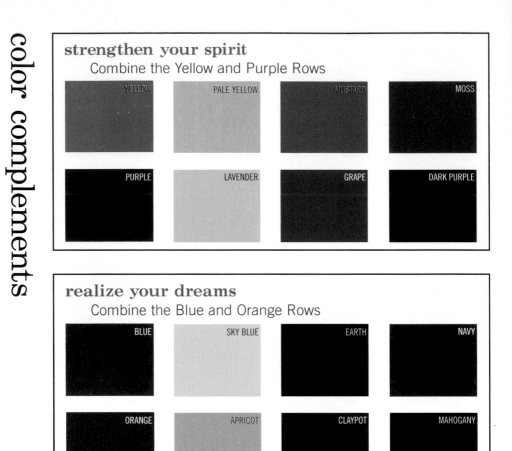

| YELLOW | PALE YELLOW | MUSTARD | MOSS |
| PURPLE | LAVENDER | GRAPE | DARK PURPLE |

realize your dreams
Combine the Blue and Orange Rows

| BLUE | SKY BLUE | EARTH | NAVY |
| ORANGE | APRICOT | CLAYPOT | MAHOGANY |

express heartfelt desires
Combine the Red and Green Rows

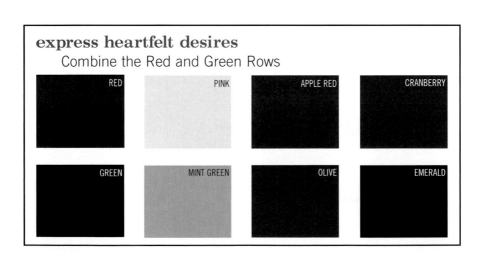

| RED | PINK | APPLE RED | CRANBERRY |
| GREEN | MINT GREEN | OLIVE | EMERALD |

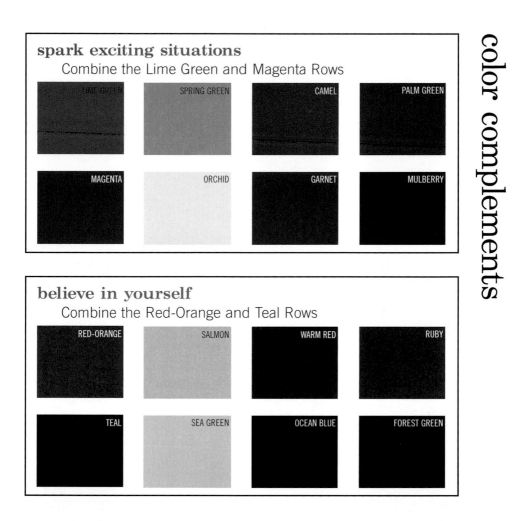

spark exciting situations
Combine the Lime Green and Magenta Rows

LIME GREEN	SPRING GREEN	CAMEL	PALM GREEN
MAGENTA	ORCHID	GARNET	MULBERRY

believe in yourself
Combine the Red-Orange and Teal Rows

RED-ORANGE	SALMON	WARM RED	RUBY
TEAL	SEA GREEN	OCEAN BLUE	FOREST GREEN

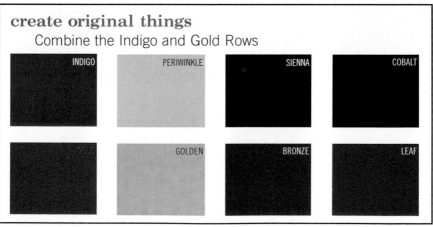

create original things
Combine the Indigo and Gold Rows

INDIGO	PERIWINKLE	SIENNA	COBALT
GOLD	GOLDEN	BRONZE	LEAF

color complements

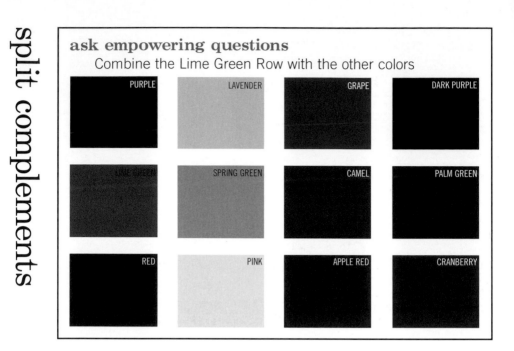

ask empowering questions
Combine the Lime Green Row with the other colors

PURPLE	LAVENDER	GRAPE	DARK PURPLE
LIME GREEN	SPRING GREEN	CAMEL	PALM GREEN
RED	PINK	APPLE RED	CRANBERRY

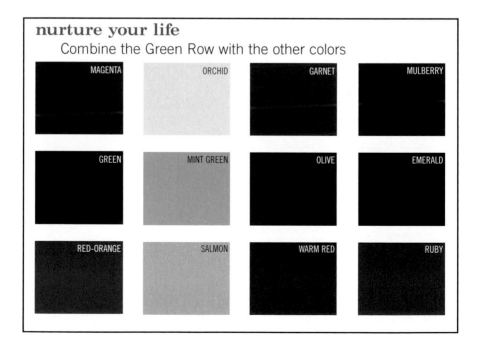

nurture your life
Combine the Green Row with the other colors

MAGENTA	ORCHID	GARNET	MULBERRY
GREEN	MINT GREEN	OLIVE	EMERALD
RED-ORANGE	SALMON	WARM RED	RUBY

split complements

appreciate your accomplishments
Combine the Teal Row with the other colors

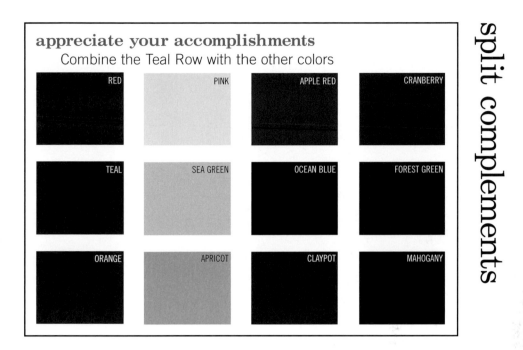

RED	PINK	APPLE RED	CRANBERRY
TEAL	SEA GREEN	OCEAN BLUE	FOREST GREEN
ORANGE	APRICOT	CLAYPOT	MAHOGANY

initiate passionate fun
Combine the Blue Row with the other colors

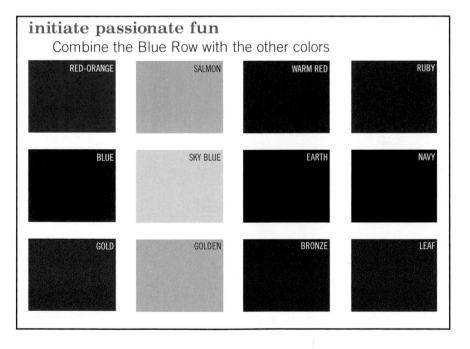

RED-ORANGE	SALMON	WARM RED	RUBY
BLUE	SKY BLUE	EARTH	NAVY
GOLD	GOLDEN	BRONZE	LEAF

create positive, workable plans
Combine the Indigo Row with the other colors

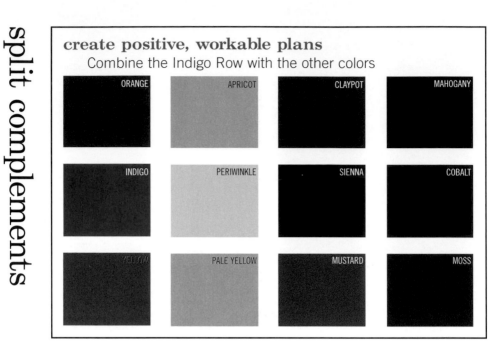

ORANGE	APRICOT	CLAYPOT	MAHOGANY
INDIGO	PERIWINKLE	SIENNA	COBALT
YELLOW	PALE YELLOW	MUSTARD	MOSS

imagine the possibilities
Combine the Purple Row with the other colors

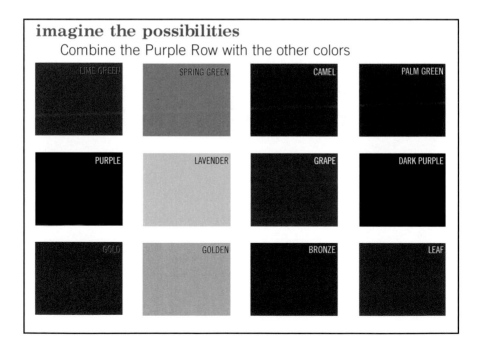

LIME GREEN	SPRING GREEN	CAMEL	PALM GREEN
PURPLE	LAVENDER	GRAPE	DARK PURPLE
GOLD	GOLDEN	BRONZE	LEAF

attract inspiring opportunities
Combine the Magenta Row with the other colors

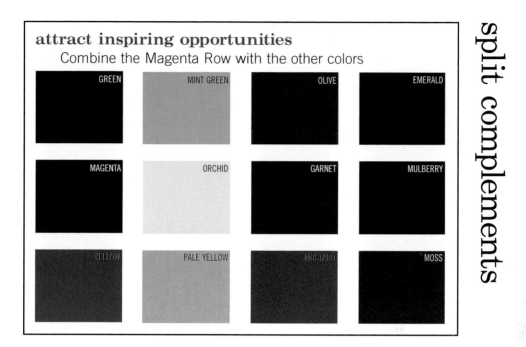

GREEN	MINT GREEN	OLIVE	EMERALD
MAGENTA	ORCHID	GARNET	MULBERRY
YELLOW	PALE YELLOW	MUSTARD	MOSS

express your effervescence
Combine the Red Row with the other colors

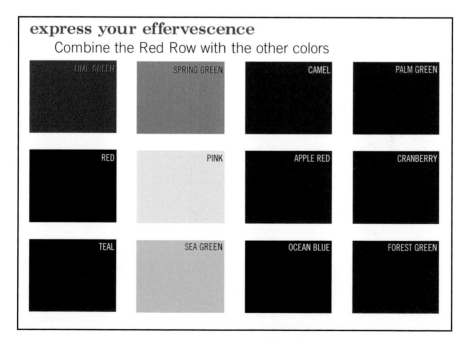

LIME GREEN	SPRING GREEN	CAMEL	PALM GREEN
RED	PINK	APPLE RED	CRANBERRY
TEAL	SEA GREEN	OCEAN BLUE	FOREST GREEN

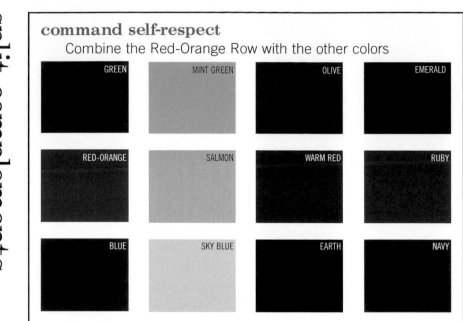

command self-respect
Combine the Red-Orange Row with the other colors

GREEN	MINT GREEN	OLIVE	EMERALD
RED-ORANGE	SALMON	WARM RED	RUBY
BLUE	SKY BLUE	EARTH	NAVY

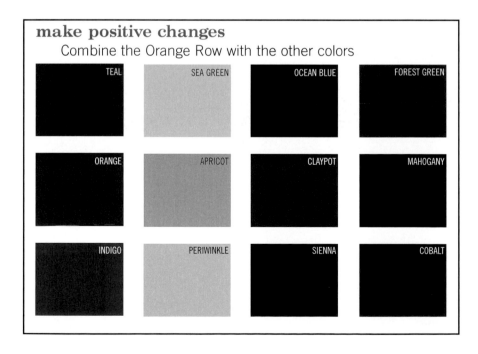

make positive changes
Combine the Orange Row with the other colors

TEAL	SEA GREEN	OCEAN BLUE	FOREST GREEN
ORANGE	APRICOT	CLAYPOT	MAHOGANY
INDIGO	PERIWINKLE	SIENNA	COBALT

split complements

playfully create a great day
Combine the Gold Row with the other colors

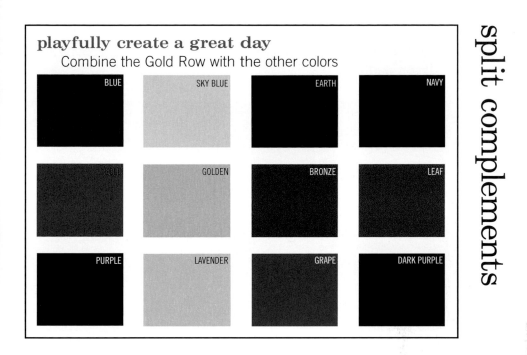

BLUE	SKY BLUE	EARTH	NAVY
GOLD	GOLDEN	BRONZE	LEAF
PURPLE	LAVENDER	GRAPE	DARK PURPLE

know your desires
Combine the Yellow Row with the other colors

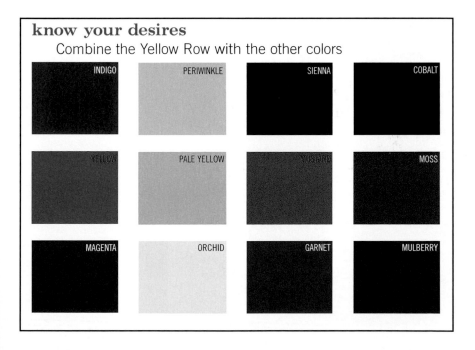

INDIGO	PERIWINKLE	SIENNA	COBALT
YELLOW	PALE YELLOW	MUSTARD	MOSS
MAGENTA	ORCHID	GARNET	MULBERRY

COLOR ENERGIZES

Give yourself a boost. Use a color that will give you pizzazz. If you want to...

question it LIME GREEN COLUMN	be it GREEN COLUMN	believe it TEAL COLUMN
dream it BLUE COLUMN	plan it INDIGO COLUMN	think it PURPLE COLUMN
inspire it MAGENTA COLUMN	express it RED COLUMN	respect it RED-ORANGE COLUMN
change it ORANGE COLUMN	play it GOLD COLUMN	know it YELLOW COLUMN
feel it BLACK COLUMN	realize it BROWN COLUMN	see it WHITE COLUMN

Refer to Chapter 15, "Muscle Up," for a more in-depth explanation.

TAKE IT SHOPPING

Don't allow your impulses to make the selection for you. Stay focused on what will fit the event or into your overall scheme. Make a mental list of your upcoming occasions. Consider the look you want or the effect you want to create in each room or outfit. Dress or decorate down a bit and be comfortable, and up a bit to be a star.

Many colors available in stores match the colors in The Dewey Color System™. Instead of looking for a certain color, loosen up. When you walk into a shop, see how you are affected by the colors on the shelves. Let the color hues embrace you.

HELPFUL SHOPPING TIP: Be especially careful of the lighting in stores. Malls, for example, have yellow lighting. So forest green, in the black row, will look more like olive, in the brown row. If there is sunlight available, take your potential purchase to the window for a color inspection.

Faded colors retain their hues, they're just not as bright. The color blue, for example, can appear as faded denim and red can appear as a faded bright pink. Even though faded, these colors will still match blue and red. Do not expect all light colors to automatically match the white column.

If a scarf, shirt, blouse, pants, or skirt has lots of colors, look beyond the printed pattern. What is the background color? Use this background color as the main color. Do not be intimidated. You can match multicolored fabrics. Most often, if the background matches, the colors will match.

CAUTION! MAKE SURE YOUR MATCH IS CORRECT. ONE SHADE OFF CAN CREATE AN UNCOORDINATED OUTFIT OR ROOM.

no mistakes

Maximize the look you want to achieve. Notice, on pages 245-255, the colors that are directly above and below each other. These vertically connected colors are no-mistake color combinations. These color best friends are not a necessity. They do, however, create a more coordinated, perfect look.

Combining a color best friend creates exciting, no-mistake combos that can pull your outfit, room, or design together with flair. For example, look at the vertical columns on page 245 to see that pale yellow, sky blue, and pink are color best friends.

choosing your colors

YOUR FAVORITE COLORS ENCOURAGE YOU TO BELIEVE IN YOUR HOPES AND ASPIRATIONS, the ideals you pursue with passion. The more you accept this passionate part of yourself, the more successful you will be. Use these colors in combinations to stimulate a new, more passionate you.

YOUR LEAST FAVORITE COLORS ARE AS SIGNIFICANT AS YOUR FAVORITE COLORS. They highlight your hidden agendas, fears, and coping mechanisms—the issues and experiences that you try to avoid. Combine these colors in combinations with your favorite colors. You will be amazed at how attached you will become to your least favorite selections. Dealing with what you would normally avoid is essential to your personal growth. It allows you to manage your life better.

ALL 60 COLORS COMBINE TO CREATE MORE THAN 3,000 STUNNING, SENSIBLE COLOR MATCHES. GO ON A COLOR SHOPPING SPREE!

embrace color vibrations

Use the language behind The Dewey Color System™ to fine-tune your color selection. By focusing on your preferences for a variety of precise color shades, you will be better able to enhance what motivates you to spark relationships, clarify decisions, solve problems, and initiate an overall higher quality of life.

Use it also to understand what a person's color preferences say about them. The Dewey Color System™ will take you on a personal empowerment journey. Turn up your color volume. Use it to personalize, yet work within, the basic rules of color in dressing and decorating.

CONSIDER THE STIMULATING EFFECT YOU WANT TO CREATE. NOW READ ABOUT IT IN THE COLOR MEANING SECTION TO SEE WHAT EACH COLOR IS GIVING YOU.

COLOR COORDINATE YOU

Whether it's for a night on the town, to make a good first impression, or just to feel good about yourself, you can, without spending big dollars, use these color combinations to boost your self-confidence and create a more focused and effective you. You will walk a little taller and be a lot bolder.

IN THIS CHAPTER

GET READY TO ENHANCE what you already have or coordinate an entirely new outfit.

LEARN HOW TO MAKE what you are wearing impact your mood or an event.

DELVE INTO THE DAILY INNER WORKING OF YOUR MIND by observing the colors you wear each day.

CREATE A NEW YOU

How you look has a lot to do with not only how you feel, but with how others see you as well. Their responses, like it or not, create your perception of yourself. Take charge of this situation. Instead of hiding inside of yourself, waiting to be discovered, use these color coordinates to become just who and what you intend.

Personal power starts with how you present yourself. Forget how you normally coordinate your wardrobe. You will gain the skills to be daring and to try new combinations. Just imagine how you could look!

go ahead—be sexy!

Look at the shape of your body. Do your hips need to be narrower? Does your chest need to be fuller? Now explore the possibility of using light and dark shades to make yourself look sexier.

Black is less, white is more. Dark colors and vertical stripes make you look thinner. Light colors and horizontal stripes make you look bigger. Separate your wardrobe into light and dark colors. For example, purple would be considered dark and yellow would be considered light.

CREATE OUTFITS THAT ENHANCE
YOUR CHEST, SCULPT YOUR WAIST,
AND SHRINK YOUR HIPS.

avoid the ughs!

Is your upper body too short or too long? Chances are you are already making adjustments according to your body type. Knowing what looks the best on you starts with knowing your body center line. Get out your measuring tape to check out your vertical balance.

MEASURE YOUR BODY CENTER LINE

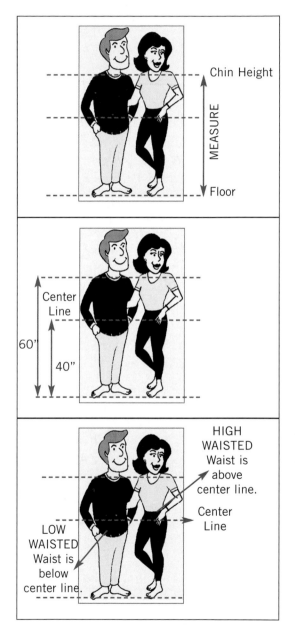

STEP 1
Measure the distance from the bottom of your chin to the floor.

STEP 2
Divide the total inches by 3. Then multiply the results by 2 to get your body center line.

STEP 3
If your waist is above the center, you are high waisted. If your waist is below the center line, you are low waisted.

BALANCE YOUR UPPER AND LOWER BODY

Don't allow your body center line to visually distract others from your overall appearance. Follow the simple adjustments below to ensure that you are looking your best.

HIGH WAISTED: Make your upper body look longer by selecting a shirt or blouse lighter than your pants or skirt. Consider wearing a belt that is the same shade as your shirt or blouse. A light shirt, for example, works well with a light belt and a dark shirt with a dark belt. Combining colors in this way will visually extend your upper body, making it appear longer. You can also wear your pants lower, or not tuck your shirt in.

LOW WAISTED: Make your upper body look shorter by selecting a shirt or blouse with horizontal stripes or one that is darker than your pants or skirt. Wear a darker shirt than your pants. Also use a belt that is the same color shade as your skirt or pants.

CENTERED: Lucky you! You can do anything you want. Everything works. For you, not wearing a belt or even wearing an outrageously fun belt looks great.

don't let the color name on the garment confuse you.
Here is an oversimplified glossary...

RED HUES: brick, chili pepper, grenadine

PINK HUES: coral, shell, watermelon, fire, orchid

GREEN HUES: kiwi, willow, mint, arctic

PURPLE HUES: eggplant, hyacinth, jasmine, glacier

YELLOW HUES: straw, sun, sunburst, dandelion

BLUE HUES: royal, sky, mist, wave, cornflower

CREATE THE PERFECT LOOK

Everyone wants to look his or her best. However, sometimes knowing what you want to look like, and what you actually do look like, are two different things. Before you coordinate colors, consider what colors look best on you. Here are a few color tips to help you find your most flattering look, while complementing your own natural features.

As you read, turn to pages 242, 243, and 244 to compare your skin, eyes, and hair color to the columns.

be captivating

Match your skin tone with the clothing that you wear next to your face. Your face will become more alive. You'll appear more inviting. Imagine that you are making a photocopy of your face. How light or dark is it? Choose a color tone that is the same tone as your skin color to be more attractive.

If you want to wear a shirt or blouse that's darker than your skin tone, choose an over shirt or jacket that's lighter. Likewise, a lighter garment than your skin tone will blend better with a darker jacket. If a color you like doesn't look good next to your face, consider an over shirt or jacket of a color that looks good on you. Your complexion will look much better.

be alluring

Match your eyes. Others will become comfortable with your very essence. Look at your eyes in a mirror under natural light. Match your eye color with a color on page 242, 243, or 244. Once you have identified a color match, look at the other colors in the column you selected. All these colors worn next to your face will make your eye color more vibrant.

BROWN EYES

Match them with either the blue, indigo, red-orange, or orange columns. If you have gold flecks, also consider the lime green and gold columns. Wear black, brown-black, sienna, or colors from the black row to make your eyes look more intense. Consider highlighting your eyes by wearing ruby, mahogany, warm red, clay pot, or colors from the brown row.

BLUE EYES

Match them with the blue column. If you have gold, green, or brown flecks, look also at the teal, indigo, and purple columns. Consider matching your eyes with the white row to show off their lightness, with the black row to make the blue brighter, and with the brown row to make them more mysterious.

GREEN EYES

Match them with green and teal. If you have gold or brown flecks consider the lime green and yellow columns. Depending upon what you wear, your eye coloring will look different. Experiment with the various colors.

eye color coordinating tips

If you want your eye color to appear lighter, more calming, use the column to the left of the one you selected. If you want your eyes to look brighter, select a color that matches your eyes. If you want them to look more intense, use one of the two columns to the right of the one you selected.

BE SEXY

Match your hair to create excitement. Look at your hair in the sunlight. Select a slightly darker or brighter shade from the column that you chose to make your hair appear more striking.

RED AND BROWN HAIR
Match with the red, red-orange, orange, and brown columns.

BLACK AND VERY DARK BROWN HAIR
Match with the blue, indigo, purple, and black columns.

BLONDE AND GRAY HAIR
Match with the gold, yellow, and white columns.

BE SEDUCTIVE

Balance your hair color to become more mysterious. Choose clothing color complements that coordinate with the color of your hair. Wearing an outfit that balances your hair color hue creates enticing harmony and makes your hair full of highlights.

RED HAIR
Balance with the lime green, green, and teal columns.

BLACK HAIR
Balance with the red-orange, orange, and gold columns.

BROWN HAIR
Balance with the teal, blue, and indigo columns.

BLONDE AND GRAY HAIR
Balance with the blue, indigo, and purple columns.

DRESSING NOTES

THE ROWS

Knowing if a color contains white, brown, or black gives you the skill to better coordinate your wardrobe. There are fifteen colors on each of the four rows. Combine each row to fit your mood or the occasion. Turn to pages 242-244.

SPECTRUM ROW: PROCLAIMS WHO YOU ARE
Use the bold matches from this row to create a statement in casual wear or at the gym. Consider combining them with the more subtle combinations (white, brown, or black shades on page 244) to make a positive first impression.

WHITE ROW: LIGHTEN UP YOUR LIFE
These combinations work well in spring and summer. Also consider using them as accessories to lighten up the day in fall and winter.

BROWN ROW: SPARK SENSATIONS
Make the fall and winter seasons a time to ground yourself. Use combinations of these colors to stir passions and communicate to others a more authentic you.

BLACK ROW: CREATE EXCITEMENT
Use the not-so-bright shades of this row to be conservative. Think about adding the brighter tones as neckties and scarves at work, or as shirts, blouses, and jackets at play. These dark colors create mystery and make you feel like you fit in.

Consider how you already coordinate your wardrobe. Chances are you are already using the basic tone agreements to pull your outfits together. Put together more combinations with less money by using the black, brown, and white columns for your basics: pants, shirts, vests, jackets, and belts.

PROCLAIM WHO YOU ARE

Wearing colors in the spectrum row will make you more colorful and your life more eventful. Some days, however, they can be too confrontational. Use the white, brown, and black columns to tone them down. Accessorize with a purple scarf, red jewelry, or a yellow jacket.

Be a star, jazz up your wardrobe. Wearing these colors will inspire you to take action. Fashion suggestions for combining lime green, indigo, and red-orange are listed below.

WOMEN, be young and chic with lime green pants, a white scoop-necked blouse or tank top, and red-orange or indigo accessories. Dress in black with a splash of color in an orange scarf on a red-orange blouse to create the vibrant expression of the sun. Be hip with a slimming indigo skirt and a taupe blouse. Accessorize with black jewelry and lime green sunglasses, belt, or purse. Be a bit dressier with a black skirt, indigo blazer, white blouse, and a red-orange or lime green scarf.

MEN, show the sexy, aggressive you by wearing casual indigo pants or shorts with a red-orange T-shirt or tank top. Be a little dressier with black pants, an indigo shirt and a red-orange sweater. Be the hit of the party with a black suit, an indigo shirt and a lime green tie.

LIGHTEN UP YOUR LIFE

Wearing colors in the white row will free you up. Use these lighter shades where you want to look bigger and the darker shades where you want to look smaller. Be careful. All these light shades will enlarge you. Consider wearing light-colored shirts, blouses, or scarves with darker pants and skirts to slim down your hips or waist.

The white row works especially well with the shades in the white column in spring and summer and in combination with the black column to create a dramatic flair in winter.

WOMEN, mix spring green, mint green, and sea green with pink, salmon, and apricot, or pale yellow with periwinkle or sky blue to create refreshing outfits. If you have slim hips, use this column to show them off. If not, consider a slimming black skirt with a desert jacket and a lavender, orchid, or sky blue blouse. Be dressy with pewter, desert, and almond combinations. Consider your options.

MEN, be casual. Wear the entire white row with slacks from the black or brown column. Consider almond or desert pants or shorts with a periwinkle or sky blue shirt. Make a tasteful statement with desert pants, a white shirt, and a pewter summer sweater. Be dressier with a sky blue jacket, pale yellow or spring green shirt, with white or black pants. Accessorize your formal black tuxedo with a sea green or lavender bow tie, or your white dinner jacket with a mint green, sky blue, or periwinkle tie.

the white row

SPARK SENSATIONS

WEARING COLORS IN THE BROWN ROW ALLOWS YOU TO BE MORE AUTHENTIC, EARTHY, AND SENSUAL. The brown row works especially well with the white column in spring and summer and in combination with the black column in winter. If you feel that these shades are too dark or too bright, use lighter shades of these hues, faded fabrics, or patterns in which these colors are the background color. Fashion suggestions for combining colors in the brown row are listed below.

WOMEN, express the casual, sensual part of you with olive jeans, a beige T-shirt or sweater, and an earth-like over shirt with camel jewelry. Create a sensation in a claypot short, fitted dress, mustard shoes and scarf, and warm red jewelry. Dress it up a bit with an ocean blue blouse, sienna skirt, bronze jacket and gold jewelry. Give the business world something to talk about with a long garnet dress or pant suit, a grape scarf, bronze jacket, and camel jewelry.

MEN, be casual and cool in a an ocean blue or a garnet shirt with beige slacks or a bronze shirt with olive slacks. Go for that unshaven look with a camel or mustard shirt, an olive jacket, and earth or camel slacks. Or be more rugged in a sienna or beige shirt with an earth-colored leather jacket and olive slacks. Get that cleaned-up look with a bronze jacket, white shirt, olive slacks, and garnet tie.

CREATE EXCITEMENT

WEARING COLORS IN THE BLACK ROW CREATES AN AIR OF MYSTERY. The black row is the most popular, especially for pants, skirts, and suits. These dark colors subdue all the other rows. They especially work well in the business world. Use the black row when you want to be more focused, or make a part of you look smaller.

WOMEN, be chic in navy dress pants and blouse, an emerald blazer, and a palm green scarf either worn around the neck, stuck in the pocket of the blazer, or wrapped as a belt. Captivate everyone at the party in a cobalt satin dress, matching cobalt satin pumps, a satin drape of leaf, moss, taupe or white, with forest green or rhinestone earrings and necklace. Light up the party with a taupe slip dress and a matching tuxedo jacket, accessorized with a dark purple scarf around the neck and sparkly mulberry gemstone jewelry.

MEN, this row is rich in color options for you to be strictly business. Wear a navy or charcoal suit with a white or sky blue shirt. Then select any color in the black row for your tie. Be trendy in a brown-black suit with a white shirt and a leaf, ruby, or a palm green tie. Classic can be fun, too, in a cobalt sports coat, taupe pants, a white button-down shirt, and a leaf or moss tie. Party in a black or charcoal tweed sports coat, pleated black wool pants, dark purple shirt, and a palm green tie.

DRESSING NOTES

THE COLUMNS

If you're looking to make dressing a simpler yet more creative process, choose a vertical column of colors. YOU'LL FIND THAT COLORS FROM THE SAME COLUMN WORK WELL WITH EACH OTHER BECAUSE THEY ARE BLENDS FROM THE SAME HUE. In spite of their different appearance, they come from the same family.

SELECT A COLUMN FROM PAGES 242-244
THAT YOU FEEL PASSIONATE ABOUT. READ THE
INTRODUCTION TO YOUR SELECTED COLUMN IN
CHAPTER 11, "HAPPINESS AND HEALING."

EXAMPLE: The lime green column on page 242 is accessorized with the black, brown, and white columns on page 244.

WOMEN, dress casual by wearing black pants with a lime green, palm green, camel, or spring green shirt. To be slightly dressier, wear a black blouse and palm green pants or skirt, accessorizing with a lime green scarf or jewelry. To be more captivating, try a spring green dress or suit with a white blouse and a camel or palm green scarf around your neck.

MEN, get a spring casual look by wearing white, black, or ivory pants with a spring green or lime green shirt. Be rugged with taupe, brown-black, or charcoal pants and a palm green shirt. Be ready for a classy evening in palm green pants, a black blazer, white shirt, and a lime green tie. Or wear a camel blazer, palm green pants, a white shirt, and a lime green or spring green tie.

dressing by columns

MAKE A STRONG REQUEST

WEARING SELECTIONS FROM THE SAME COLOR CATEGORY COLUMNS SHOWS A SPECIFIC REQUEST. For example, wearing blue and red shades together from the primary category can create this effect. Color theorists call these matches triadic.

VIEW THE TRIADIC COMBINATIONS
ON PAGES 245, 246, AND 247.

Combine any of the 12 colors in each grouping to create vibrant, directive energy. Use colors from the same vertical columns to achieve an even more balanced combination. Seek a seductive response with the achromatic combination examples below.

WOMEN, wear hip-slimming black pants with a brown or white blouse. Then, add a brown-black jacket with a brown or white scarf. Or be sensual in a tan leather skirt, a desert-colored top, a taupe wrap and no jewelry. Get serious and still be sexy in a black cat suit and jacket, and accessorize with silver (a lighter shade of taupe) necklace and earrings. Capture your mate with a black silk dress, silver strapless high-heeled sandals, a silver necklace and bracelet, or a pewter scarf tied in a back knot around your neck.

MEN, work it for all you can. Wear slimming black jeans, pants, or shorts. Add the excitement of high contrast with a white, taupe, or beige shirt, preferably with horizontal stripes to make your chest look wider. The lighter the shirt, the more powerful your chest looks. Get dressed up in a brown-black suit or a brown-black sports coat with black pants, a white shirt, and a tie with a black, pewter, or taupe background.

Wear the black, brown, and white columns to send a sexy message. Black says you are a challenge, brown intimates that you need to feel sensations, and white indicates that you are looking for someone or something new.

CREATE HARMONY

Wearing selections from the spectrum opposites creates more color yet still looks very together. THESE COMBINATIONS WILL CREATE A FEELING OF BALANCE.

When you coordinate with color complements, you will be amazed at how unobtrusive they really are. Even the brightest of colors will become more subdued. In fact, you might have to spark them up by mixing lighter and darker tones together. Try matching your least favorite color with its color opposite. You will feel even more balanced.

VIEW THESE COLOR COORDINATES
ON PAGES 248 AND 249.

WOMEN, use the yellow and purple columns to be casually alluring. Consider, for example, wearing moss shorts, a mustard shirt, and a lavender lightweight cotton sweater. Be a little dressier by creating an outfit using the indigo and gold columns. Wear a periwinkle skirt with a leaf blouse and a golden scarf.

MEN, be more fun by selecting from the blue and orange columns. Wear navy shorts or pants with an apricot shirt. Turn it up a notch using the lime green and magenta columns, matching a palm green blazer, black pants, taupe shirt, and a mulberry tie. Dress for success in a cobalt suit and periwinkle shirt from the indigo column, accessorized with a tie from any of the colors in the orange column.

SPARK VIBRANT ENERGY

Get ready for, "Wow, who was that?" If you have the courage to be original, here is your chance to shine. SPLIT COMPLEMENTS CREATE A MORE TRENDY, FASHIONABLE LOOK. You can subdue these overwhelming combinations with either the black, white, or brown column, or by not using the spectrum row.

VIEW THESE COORDINATES
ON PAGES 250-255.

Look at the top box of color coordinates on page 250. Combine the lime green row with either the purple or red row to ask empowering questions.

WOMEN, express your charming, strictly business side in a tailored pink suit with a spring green camisole, brightened with a teal scarf containing a pink and spring green print. To captivate your audience, wear a cranberry dress with camel jewelry and forest green shoes and purse. For a dressy casual look for summer, wear a soft fabric dress in a lime green print, possibly floral, with forest green or red sandals, and accessorize with earrings of forest green and red.

MEN, be dressy casual in forest green pants, a camel blazer, white shirt, and a cranberry, apple red, or pink tie. Be funky casual with palm green, ocean blue, or camel pants matched with a pink, apple red, or red shirt. Dress it up with a forest green, ocean blue, camel, or palm green blazer along with black pants and a white shirt. Select your tie color from the red column.

WHY DID YOU WEAR THAT COLOR TODAY?

Are you wearing red? Why? Why not sky blue? Perhaps you woke up this morning and found yourself gravitating toward a certain color. While this may feel like an unconscious decision, it's actually your subconscious mind guiding you to the color that will help you through your day—to conquer the moment.

IF YOU ARE ATTRACTED TO A CERTAIN COLOR SHADE TODAY, READ ABOUT IT.

If you have a choice, what you wear each day reveals where you need to give yourself a boost. For instance, if you wear the green shades, you have a need to be nurtured. If you wear the red shades, you have a need to be expressive. If you are wearing a multicolored fabric, notice what color in the pattern stands out the most. If you are wearing lots of colors, what color dominates or is next to your face? If you are dressed in a conservative suit, what color is your tie or scarf?

ARE YOU WEARING YOUR FAVORITE COLORS TODAY? These colors reassure you. They will make you feel that, for the most part, everything is okay. You will become more focused. Wearing your favorite colors is a sign that little things will not distract you from your goals.

ARE YOU WEARING YOUR LEAST FAVORITE COLORS TODAY? If so, you are going to create excitement by confronting areas that you normally avoid. Using the color shades in your least favorite color selection columns can heal specific areas of your life.

WHAT ARE OTHERS WEARING? Look around you. Read about them. What do they need today? Use this vital information to enhance your approach. You'll find that others will listen more intently, and odds are you'll stand a better chance of getting what you want.

14

COLOR YOUR WORLD

In all of us there is an exciting new world waiting to be discovered. Look around. Especially at home! Couldn't your rooms be more alive? Drab and boring surroundings make you feel tired. Color gives energy. Get excited. It's time for a change in your life. It's time to shake up your living environment with a burst of fresh color!

IN THIS CHAPTER

BREAK FROM YOUR TRADITIONAL WALL COLOR, FABRIC, AND ACCESSORY COLOR PREJUDICES! It doesn't have to be uncomfortable. In fact, it can be tremendously liberating. Use the tone agreement of this system to take new steps.

YOU WILL LEARN HOW TO MAKE EACH ROOM IN YOUR HOME A REFLECTION OF YOUR INNER PASSION. Color has the power to transform your space into a sacred place. Your self-esteem and well-being will soar.

PASSIONATE COLORS ARE CONTAGIOUS

Do you want to increase passion in your bedroom, culinary energy in your kitchen, or learning in your study? Passionate colors are contagious. You can make your lover more emotional, more energized, or more physical. Or consider creating an environment where your child will be more goal-oriented. It's time you started thinking about color—vibrant, kinetic color to help you become more spiritual, sensual, and adventurous.

before you begin

A sense of comfort is what makes a house a home. If you live with other people or have frequent guests, you should pull everyone together and take a survey of what sort of environment they would like to live in.

How do you use your house? Take a walk around. View each room separately. Where will you, your friends, and family sit to watch TV or read? Can you see the TV from the living room sofa? Consider where your telephone lines are. Is the chair you are going to buy comfortable? Will the carpet last? How well will it endure stains? When you are in bed, what is your view? Is there a better way to position the bed? What size bath mat fits the bathroom and allows you to close the door?

Ask these and other practical questions before you get creative. Remembering to get everyone on the same page and to understand what needs have to be met will save you a lot of headaches.

create the magic

Give each room a theme that conveys the feelings you want. Look at the style of your home in general. What themes will work?

Do you want your room to be cozy, funky, or formal? Perhaps you'd like to recreate the look of a certain period or place. Are you thinking Southwestern, Roman, French, or Italian? Why not something Art Nouveau or modern? Anything is possible. You might want to recreate the look of your childhood and go with something from the 70's, 60's, 50's—maybe even the 20's!

Consider how you would feel if you adopted each theme. Then select the theme that sparks the most passion. Would you prefer to feel more exotic, intellectually stimulated, more adventuresome, more playful, or more focused? Remember, your objective is to add new life to your world. Don't hold back. Life is short and time is moving on.

AESTHETICS 101

Look at the shape of your room. Start with the walls. Use light or dark colors to create more comfortable shapes. White makes rooms look larger. Darker shades will bring the walls in. Mirrors at right angles to the window will give maximum light reflectance and double the size of the space.

the long wall

Don't put any furniture against this wall. Instead, hang a mirror, as large as possible, on the wall or mirror the entire wall. Glass on framed pictures reflects light as well, making your room feel more open.

the short wall

On the short wall, place pictures, furniture, or accents in a darker color. You will bring the room in, making the short and long walls feel more balanced.

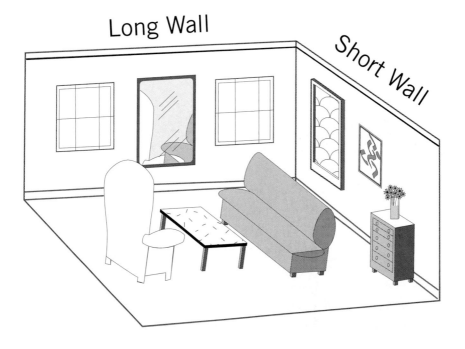

ceiling height

TO MAKE YOUR CEILING SEEM HIGHER, paint it white or use a lighter tint of the wall color. Also, keep the floors light. An off-white rug will increase ceiling height, and it's easier to clean than you might think. Paint the molding the same color tone as the room, not darker or lighter. Darker walls and long vertical mirrors and pictures will also give your ceiling more height. Do not add designs or details that call attention to the ceiling.

TO MAKE YOUR CEILING LOWER, paint your ceiling darker than the room or paint the molding a darker color. Horizontal-shaped mirrors and pictures will also seem to give your ceiling less height. Making use of borders and designs will create an exciting impact and give your rooms a sense of detail. Darker area rugs will also add to making the space cozier.

examine every color

Examine every existing color in the room that you will not or cannot change, such as the color of the wood floors, carpets, expensive furniture pieces, and any vases or existing art you may want to use. Which colors blend with the room? Which colors highlight? For example, orange tones bring out dark wooden furniture, doors, or floors. If you are using wallpaper, be aware of the background color. It will dominate.

It's also a good idea to check out any possible color schemes in both natural and artificial light. Daylight will highlight objects nearest to the windows, leaving the rest of the room in progressively deeper shadows as you move away from the windows. If the room is not too deep and contains only one window, the wall facing will be brighter than the sides and the window wall.

At night, however, the room is likely to be more evenly lit. Use several light sources to ensure that all the surfaces, and hence the colors and textures, are seen more clearly. Halogen and low-voltage halogen bulbs emit a bright white light, which renders colors truer, while common incandescent bulbs emit warmer light.

THE ROWS

Coordinating colors creates a world that's all your own. By combining the colors from each row you can make stunning statements in your home about the way you feel. In addition, you can challenge the way others see you. There are many possible combinations.

TURN TO PAGES 242-244 TO
SEE THE SPECTRUM, WHITE,
BROWN, AND BLACK ROWS.

FIRST: Select the row you prefer most, or the one that already goes with the colors that you are using.

SECOND: Consider how you want to feel in each room. Review the color possibilities in the shopping guide.

recreate nature

Use these natural blends to create nature. Combine salmon, apricot, and golden in the white row to make a vibrant sunburst; create an autumn morning with bronze, mustard, and camel from the brown row; or a sultry forest with emerald, palm green, and forest green in the black row. Imagine the possibilities!

decorating with rows

CREATE PASSION

BY COORDINATING COLORS IN THE SPECTRUM ROW, YOU'LL BETTER EXPRESS YOURSELF. A room using these bright colors might be easier to live in than you think. Consider making the walls white. Now, imagine that you're a decorator using only the colors in this row. What color would you make the bedspread, chair, sofa, vase, or curtains?

NOTE: BE CAREFUL—THE BRIGHTER SHADES IN THIS ROW CAN KEEP YOU FROM SLEEPING.

These vivid colors work especially well as accessories. They can make a dull room zing. Simply look at the colors already in the room. Now either row or column coordinate one of these colors with another color in the spectrum row. Pillows, towels, and rugs allow for splashes of bright colors. Go ahead. Turn on the lights!

express yourself

Consider making a room off the living room, a place where you can really enjoy life. Below is an example of a garden room theme using the spectrum row.

Paint the walls green or white. Install a black and white alternating tile floor or select a carpet color with a combination of the shades from the white column to hide stains.

Show the expressive you with a purple couch, two red leather chairs, accessorized with lime green pillows and knickknacks. Add green plants in white urns, and you'll become immersed in a world where you can express your essence.

CREATE FREEDOM

USE THE COLORS IN THE WHITE ROW TO CREATE MORE FREEDOM. Consider using these colors on your walls, bedspreads, or curtains. They will create more space and open up your world. This will increase your objectivity and enable you to see new options. You will feel cooler, not confined. Your new freedom will lighten up your life.

Mary Ann Petro, a well-known color design expert, has created examples using the white row. Her design works with many themes and lets the sun shine into your home. To give your spirit a sense of freedom, Ms. Petro avoids restrictive dark shades and black. The trim for the entire house, all windows, and the molding for each room are painted a high-gloss white.

let the sunshine in

For your foyer, use a semi-gloss golden color on the walls and a table in an antique white. Accessorize with a gold-framed picture and mirror. In the living room, try a lighter shade of pale yellow for the walls. This gives a sun-washed effect. A floral, multicolored chintz fabric is a great idea for the furniture and pillows. Choose a rug in a pale yellow design.

Give faces a more glamorous glow by painting the dining room walls a lighter shade of salmon. Consider periwinkle on the ceiling and rug. Make the kitchen walls, molding, cabinets, and table white. This will make the colors and textures of the food more mouth-watering. You'll be able to enliven the room with your linens, flowers, and table settings.

Create your own private world with a bedroom that has orchid on the walls and a sky blue ceiling. Use orchid, spring green, and white for the bedspread. Consider making her bathroom a lighter shade of orchid and his bathroom a lighter shade of spring green.

CREATE SENSATION

COMBINE THE COLORS IN THE BROWN ROW TO EMBRACE SENSATIONS AND STIMULATE TOUCH, SMELL, AND TASTE. What do you want right now? How do you want to feel? Combining colors from this column will make you more relaxed and comfortable living in your space.

Consider painting your room lighter shades of these colors. You will be shocked with the delicate warmth that they radiate. You will find that even the lighter tones from this row create warmth. Use them to make your dining room more appetizing, bathroom more sensual, or TV room more comfortable.

This row works especially well in rooms where you want to feel grounded. These shades blend with naturally stained doors, floors, or wooden furniture. Use them to bring your room together.

drink knowledge

Below is an example of a library using the sensuous, relaxing colors of the brown row.

Paint the walls beige, olive, or a lighter shade of mustard. Select or stain your desk, bookcases, and chairs with a shade of sienna. Cover the chairs or sofa in olive or ocean blue, or do your desk chairs in one color and your sitting area in the other. Then accessorize with claypot pillows and camel statues. Now, sit behind your desk or relax in one of your chairs and drink from the intoxicating fountain of knowledge.

CREATE DRAMA

COORDINATE YOUR ROOMS WITH COLORS IN THE BLACK ROW TO STIMULATE ADVENTURES AND EMPOWERING THOUGHTS. Using these colors will also help you focus on your goals.

These colors don't have to be dark. When selecting a wall color, for example, simply get out the sample paint chips and pick a lighter shade of the same hue. Don't be alarmed at the brightness of this new shade. It will blend marvelously with all the other colors in the black row.

Consider a room where you sit and work, do your thinking, or become enthralled by your favorite music. Wouldn't you prefer colors that help your ideas flow?

take a jungle ride

Below is an example of a cozy TV room with a jungle theme using the black row. The contrast of light walls and dark furniture enhances the drama.

Paint the walls taupe or a light shade of forest green. Select a forest green sofa with emerald and palm green pillows to create the natural lush tones of nature. Add mahogany-stained chairs with apricot, orange, or a dark purple fabric. Then accessorize with a dark purple piece of amethyst or cobalt vases and pottery. Pictures of wild animals on the walls will give your room an even more adventurous zip. Then, get crazy! Take a trip inside your imagination. Enter the dark jungle of your mind and you just might find yourself really entertaining.

DECORATING NOTES

THE COLUMNS

Since the blends within each column are from the same color hue, these color combinations pull a room together. Your wall colors, sofas, and pillows will just seem to fit. Select a column that you feel passionate about.

VIEW ALL 15 COLUMNS ON PAGES 242-244.
READ THE INTRODUCTION TO YOUR SELECTED COLUMN
IN CHAPTER 11, "HAPPINESS AND HEALING."

in this section

If you're using multicolored fabrics, throw rugs, oriental carpets, or even paintings, you'll be amazed! They will follow one of the classic design patterns in this section.

ACCESSORIZE WITH THE ACHROMATIC COLUMNS
* BROWN column to be more authentic, earthy, and sensual
* WHITE column to be more open
* BLACK column to better know yourself

pull your room together

These combinations work especially well in difficult or chopped up spaces. If you have a room that has lots of doorways or points of interest, such as a fireplace, large bed, or TV, consider using color tones predominantly from one column to pull the room together.

Also consider coordinating the natural wood or leather tones in your room with brighter shades in the same column to make your floors, doors, paneling, or leather furniture come alive. For example, mahogany works well with the orange, red-orange, and red columns, and sienna with the blue, indigo, and purple columns.

decorating with columns

CREATE POWER ROOMS

THESE STRONG HUES CAN REALLY MAKE A STATEMENT. Create a strong statement by selecting combinations that energize you, your children, or spouse.

COMBINE TWO OF THE THREE
ROWS ON PAGES 245, 246, AND 247
TO CREATE VIBRANT ENERGY.

make work fun

Below is an example of a crisp, sharp home office that will be conducive to accomplishing your goals. Create it by using combinations within the yellow, blue, and red columns. View these color combinations at the top of page 245.

Paint the walls a pale yellow or a bright white. Buy a new navy desk or paint your existing desk. Then cover your desk chair in a moss fabric with a moss or navy set of chairs or a sofa. Add red pillows and accessories to give this original design the vibrant energy you need to make your dreams a reality.

OPEN UP YOUR WORLD

CONSIDER USING THESE COLOR COMPLEMENTS IN PLACES WHERE YOU WANT TO FEEL MORE SECURE, LIKE A BEDROOM OR A COZY STUDY.

VIEW THE COMPLEMENTS
ON PAGES 248 AND 249.

Exciting shadows will appear when you combine the light and dark shades within the two columns that you have selected. You might, for example, place an orange glass vase on a sky blue shelf or windowsill, or combine dark purple and pale yellow to create a lively combo.

create a garden

Below is an example of a harmonic bedroom with a garden room theme. Using shades of the red and green columns at the bottom of page 248, you can better express your heartfelt desires.

Select a floral print fabric that contains mostly colors from these columns. Then accessorize with colors from the print. Floral patterns do not have to be feminine; abstract designs may give the impression of flowers. Paint the walls a bright, semi-gloss white or mint green and, if you like, make the molding stand out with a high-gloss white.

Use a white bedspread with a floral print dust ruffle and add pillows to match the dust ruffle. Curtains can be a floral print or white with a border of the floral fabric at the bottom. Add red leather chairs or a red leather sofa. Then, take it another step. Let your artwork and books give added comfort to the soulful, rejuvenating powers of your private garden.

FEEL ENERGIZED—MORE ALIVE

Color theorists tell us that we can create bold and exciting energy by selecting a color one shade off the spectrum opposites. THESE SPLIT COMPLEMENTS WILL FIRE UP YOUR ROOMS. They are the ultimate expression in the color spectrum.

VIEW THE IMPACT OF EACH OF
THE TWELVE SPLIT COMPLEMENTS
ON PAGES 250-255.

Imagine these color combinations in your living room, bedroom, TV room, or on your patio. Use them for new spaces or to accessorize with a row or color that you have already selected. These combinations will really jazz up a bland room.

enjoy the day

Below is an example of a living room with the theme of the early 1900's, using the blue column exploding with the red-orange and gold columns. View these combinations at the bottom of page 251. Ensure that in color coordinating the split complements, you view the red-orange and gold shades in combinations with the blue shades.

Paint the walls or the ceiling sky blue. For the windows, select off-white or white Venetian styled draperies with gold trim or even tassels. Add two navy chairs, with an off-white or rugged earth leather sofa. Accessorize with red-orange pillows. Then fill the room with shiny brass vases, statues, or whatever gold-colored things you like. Finally, let that bygone charm take you back to more serene times.

MUSCLE UP

You need all the colors. Muster the courage to cherish and embrace all 15 of them. Use them as your guide. You will gain strength—a more centered, stronger inner balance. Your new awareness will give you the muscle to make your life a passionate adventure.

You are nearing the end of your self-empowering journey. Consider, as you read, how the unspoken power of each color affects the complicated issues in your life.

IN THIS CHAPTER

VIEW THE COLORS YOU PREFER TO SEE YOUR STRENGTHS. Look again, you will also see where you are stubborn, even arrogant.

VIEW THE COLORS YOU LEAST PREFER TO CELEBRATE WHAT YOUR PAST EXPERIENCES HAVE TAUGHT YOU. They will also indicate the areas of your life where you feel uncomfortable.

TRUTH IS SIMPLE

Truth is always simple. If you think that you are complicated, chances are you are avoiding the fascinating inner workings that make up you. Stay focused on how you feel, not on what you think, do, or even what others say.

Don't let past experiences cloud your perspective. If you feel a relationship or situation is difficult to understand, you are not aware of, or accepting, all of the facts.

empower your conversation

The goal of The Dewey Color System™ is to give you an awareness of how you prioritize your life. In learning the rewards and consequences of the way you set priorities, you gain the power to manage and direct your personality, focus on your passions, and realize your potential.

Create a real conversation. Talk with your children, spouse, parents, or team members at work about their colors. Understanding how they prioritize their lives will allow you to be more patient about things that bother you and more appreciative of what they contribute.

the color countdown

You are about to experience the color countdown, a condensed, in-depth summary of all 15 colors. Your colors and life priorities are the same. Color was simply used as a way to access YOU, without the interference of language.

In reviewing the great power of each color in The Dewey Color System™, feel the passion and power within you. Use this spectrum-ordered summary to better link your thoughts and increase your quality of life.

As you read the color countdown, constantly be aware of the order in which you selected your colors. It determines your process of creating empowering change within yourself. You will gain insightful clues that will give you the awareness to better direct and manage your life.

THE 15 GREAT POWERS

LIME GREEN	**question it**™
GREEN	**be it**™
TEAL	**believe it**™
BLUE	**dream it**™
INDIGO	**plan it**™
PURPLE	**think it**™
MAGENTA	**inspire it**™
RED	**express it**™
RED-ORANGE	**respect it**™
ORANGE	**change it**™
GOLD	**play it**™
YELLOW	**know it**™
BLACK	**feel it**™
BROWN	**realize it**™
WHITE	**see it**™

"The aim of life is self-development.
To realize one's nature perfectly—that is
what each of us is here for. People are
afraid of themselves, nowadays."

OSCAR WILDE

POWER NOTES

LIME GREEN POWER

Lime green gives you the stamina to question what is missing in your life. Ignite your passions by letting your inner voice speak. You will discover how you are yearning to feel. Questioning yourself gives you the power to know exactly what you need to do.

Exploring your thoughts is not the same as embracing them. Don't be afraid to confess your hidden, shocking considerations. They are simply clues to understanding yourself.

lime green and you

THE MORE YOU LIKE LIME GREEN, the more you question what is missing in your life.

THE LESS YOU LIKE LIME GREEN, the more you avoid confronting what is missing in your life.

look beyond your shocking thoughts

Thoughts like, "I need a divorce," "No one loves me," or "I am lazy," are not necessarily how you really feel. Look beyond. Consider your inner needs. Learning what makes you passionate will fire up your engine.

Everything starts—and ends—with you. You can search the world over, moving from one city to another, to no avail. No matter where you go, you will create the same world again. Knowing your desires creates aggressive, positive energy. Others will see you as exciting—they will feel that they know you, even when they first meet you.

question it ™

sweep out the cobwebs

Complete every thought before you move to the next. If you don't, you will become scattered. Think about how it would feel if you actually did what you are thinking. Now think again. Do you really need it? Make your mind razor sharp. Complete each thought or discussion with yourself.

GREEN POWER

Green gives you a stronger understanding of yourself. Be true to the child in you by taking the time to make sure the "me" in you is okay. You will obtain the power of inner strength, able to create a more nurturing, supportive world.

Visit with this very real you by forgetting, for the moment, your immediate wants and others. Only you will exist. You will be able to listen for what makes you or others comfortable. Your greater awareness will give you the power to be yourself or detect what others really need to be themselves.

green and you

THE MORE YOU LIKE GREEN, the more aware you are of the support that you and others need.

THE LESS YOU LIKE GREEN, the more unaware you are about what you and others need to be supported.

find a refuge

Find a park, beach, a special room, or a quiet cafe where you can monitor the conversation you are having with yourself. What do you really want? Be specific. What are you getting? Losing? Don't hold back. Bring all your forbidden wants to the surface. Dwelling on them is a waste of your time and energy.

Get to know the "me" within you. Make every thought start with "me." Consider this "me" thought: "I am helping my friend because I want her to succeed," instead of, "She is in trouble so I have to help her." You are doing, for the most part, what you want to do. Own it and you will see the contributions you are giving to the world.

be responsible

Making your life just about you can be very exciting—and frightening. All of a sudden you are responsible for just yourself. If your feeling of being needed makes it difficult to be at peace with such a selfish thought, look deeper. Talk to yourself like a small child. You will become comfortable visiting with just you.

Everyone is happier when you tell them what you want. Don't be so polite. Many times it is only a mechanism to avoid confronting yourself or a situation. Tell yourself exactly what you want out of life.

become a great listener

Allow your thoughts to be just about the other person. You will gain the power to listen for who they are, before you consider yourself. Giving someone else your full attention is a great compliment. You will make them feel comfortable—able to be themselves. Oops! All of a sudden you will also see who they really need to be.

consider your favorite color

Now write down your favorite color and list three adjectives that describe why you like it.

Favorite Color   Adjectives

_____   1. _____
                                              2. _____
                                              3. _____

Doesn't this describe what you need to be yourself? Now, look around. Where are you getting it? Not getting it?

TEAL POWER

Teal inspires you to believe in your wishes. Get intense. Wish over and over until you believe in your capacity to accomplish your dreams. Believe in your wish and you will gain the power to believe in yourself.

Don't judge yourself by who you are now. You are also who you dream to be! Ask others about their dreams. Now close your eyes and visualize your own dream. Become inspired.

teal and you

THE MORE YOU LIKE TEAL, the more you can appreciate your progress in attaining your dreams.

THE LESS YOU LIKE TEAL, the more difficult it is for you to feel that you are capable of achieving your dreams.

talk up your day

What you tell yourself is very powerful. Ask yourself, when you awake, "What makes me passionate?" After breakfast, "What can I do, or not do, today?" At the day's end, "What great things did I do today?"

Constantly acknowledge what you are accomplishing and you can even flip a negative situation into a positive, constructive adventure. Believe in your capabilities and nothing will be able to slow you down.

dance every day

When you listen to a song, you hear the melody and then the words. Let your passion for doing what you want to do be the melody in your life. Tune in to yourself and even your slowest songs will develop a distinctive upbeat tempo. After a while, you'll be dancing.

Protect the rhythm in your spirit. It will allow you to appreciate what you accomplish. Ask yourself, "Who am I?" Write down your thoughts. Constantly proclaim them every morning when you arise. You will become a believer in yourself—better able to accomplish your dream.

who do you aspire to be?

Name a person you most admire. Now list three adjectives that reflect why you admire this person. Record your responses below.

Person You Admire   Adjectives

_____   1. _____
                                                           2. _____
                                                           3. _____

Isn't this also who you aspire to be? If not, look again. Are you trying to please someone else more than yourself? Stop pretending. Make your own wish.

BLUE POWER

Blue gives you the focus to visualize. Expand your mind by concentrating on your future. Dream. You will gain the power of mental discipline and be able to envision a more beautiful life.

Make a definite goal. Constantly considering your future will keep you on the right road. Focus, focus, focus. Do not relent until you become your aspiration. Others will see your courage as self-confidence and want to be on your team.

blue and you

THE MORE YOU LIKE BLUE, the more optimistic you are that your dreams will work.

THE LESS YOU LIKE BLUE, the more pessimistic you are that your dreams will work.

take the ultimate risk

Don't be shy. Say that you will do what you dream. Remember a time in your life when you really pushed yourself to go beyond what you believed you could do? Wasn't it exciting? Create this energized feeling again. Say you will make your dream a reality. The anticipation of your dream will inspire you. Your life will have a sense of magic.

Take your dreams to the next level. Don't be influenced by the situation or your desires. Make your own course. Stay on your diet, cut down or eliminate smoking, and don't call back the jerk that you miss.

be conclusive

Finish every thought by eliminating the clutter of too many friends, expectations, or situations that demand your attention. They will drain your mental energy. Do one thing at a time. Take command of your future. Finish each goal.

feel your future

Today's dreams are tomorrow's actions. Be aware of your feelings and thoughts. When you feel uncomfortable, chances are something is not working. Don't be so concerned with the answers, but with the questions that need to be asked. Let them be your guide to success. Don't hesitate. Remember, no commitment equals no decision.

Statements like, "My objective is..." will keep you on track. You will see the important details. Be flexible. Listen first for how a suggestion is like yours before you see how it is different. It will make you smart—able to get the job done well and in less time.

proclaim all your dreams

Say all your dreams. Spell them out by filling in the blanks below.

Career: In five years I will be_____
_____.

In ten years I will be_____
_____.

Relationships: I will surround myself with_____
_____.
(List those you respect and who respect you.)

Spiritual: I will be more true to myself by respecting my ability to be_____,_____, and_____.
(List your strongest qualities.)

INDIGO POWER

Indigo gives you enlightened perspectives to create successful plans. Dive into each ingredient you might need to create your idea. You will gain the power to create an orchestrated, exciting future.

Establish an unrelenting focus by dwelling on exactly how you can accomplish your plan, not whether or not you can do it. Dedicate your thoughts to concentrating on why you need to do each thing and you will be able to adopt a better or easier way—a shortcut.

indigo and you

THE MORE YOU LIKE INDIGO, the more you believe in your ability to conceptualize new ideas.

THE LESS YOU LIKE INDIGO, the harder it is to believe that you need to make a plan.

be on the ball

Stay ahead of your deadlines by paying your bills on time, deciding in advance what you will cook for dinner, or with whom you will spend your time. Take charge of your life or it will take charge of you. Plan ahead. You will gain the opportunity to create the future that you desire.

Get out a calendar. Write down what you will do each day to improve your relationships, have fun, or increase the size of your bank account. Sacrificing your time today will create a successful tomorrow. Invest in yourself. You can acquire wealth, perhaps a lovely home, or even better relationships.

plan it™

Plan a New You

Create a vision of your future. List three goals you want to achieve this year.

1._____
2._____
3._____

Now, make a plan for each one. For example:

<u>My Goals</u>   <u>My Plans</u>

   1. A fun career   Focus on finding a new job
   2. A deeper inner peace   Care more about others
   3. More money   Spend less and invest

1._____
2._____
3._____

The secret to staying focused is to get excited about your plan, not the goal. Assume you can do it and your concerns will shift. They will become more conclusive. Others' opinions and current dilemmas will bother you less.

PURPLE POWER

Purple creates the ability to see new possibilities, ideas, and strategies for yourself and others. Visit with your emotions. In them you will discover a greatness that can only be imagined. You will gain the personal power to create something original.

Fight for what you believe. Don't be in a rush. Imagine that you have five years to accomplish your goals. Now what are the possibilities? Get emotional. Address your limitations beforehand so that you'll have no reservations. Once you've done this, go ahead full force, with all your heart. It will happen no matter what.

purple and you

THE MORE YOU LIKE PURPLE, the more prone you are to contemplation and self-examination.

THE LESS YOU LIKE PURPLE, the more likely you are to deny your capabilities.

be true to yourself

Allow time for silence. Create a quiet space to hear the inner voices in your head. No, you are not crazy and those voices are not aliens trying to direct your life. They are your emotions. Listen to the why, not what they are saying.

Tune in to hearing the excitement in your own voice. It will reveal what you really love to do—which, of course, is what you will do best. Now look around you. Imagine who else you can be. Be courageous. Consider all your possibilities. Let your heart, not your head, speak. You will awaken the giant within you.

create a win-win situation

Deal from the top of the deck by bringing all the issues to the table. Examine your motivations. Now look at the other person's perspective or what the situation dictates. Only then can you reach a compromise. Stay motivated. Talk about what you think, and get others to do the same.

Failure occurs only when you give up. Even a definite NO can later be a YES. When you are rejected or can't get what you want, consider why you really wanted it. Now, look around. Where else can you get it? Keep looking until you find the same or a better way. Never give up and you will never fail.

MAGENTA POWER

Magenta enthusiastically inspires you to start something new. When you are open to the world, your world will be open to you. Like a magnet, you will gain the power to attract a new opportunity.

Create a spark. Start by discarding your skeptical thoughts. Focus instead on how exciting a person or place could be. Allow your curiosity and the quest for something entirely new to rule the moment. Your exciting new body language will positively attract whatever you desire.

magenta and you

THE MORE YOU LIKE MAGENTA, the more you are inspired by your environment.

THE LESS YOU LIKE MAGENTA, the more suspicious you are of new things.

smile

A smile is inspiring. It creates exciting new situations. Remembering the fun you had on past adventures can jump-start your day. Simply allow your natural curiosity for something new to surface. Others will feel it. Your feelings will attract the adventure you are seeking.

Make each day exciting. Let the world entertain you, but don't go overboard. Make sure that what you feel is what you desire. Enthusiasm is powerful. It can even start things that you never intended.

how often do you start things?

★ Get a mirror and put it next to your telephone.

★ Look at your expressions when you talk.

★ Are you smiling all the time? OOPS! Things just seem to happen!

★ Are you never smiling? Lighten up! Don't be so suspicious.

big smiles win

Your body language is actually more powerful than what you say. For fun, play this game with a friend. Look at them and say with a big smile on your face, "You are a jerk." If you are giving them a really big smile, they will smile back!

If you are having a bad time at a party, it's usually all about you. Walk in the bathroom or away from the crowd. Discard your negative, all-about-me thoughts. Now, practice smiling and return. Look around. Become curious about someone. Give them a big smile from your heart and the fun will begin.

RED POWER

Red gives you the practical knowledge and expressive power to direct your life. Speak up. Tell the world who you are and what you want. You will gain the power to make your life and things around you work.

Be specific. Let others know what they can expect from you and what you are expecting from them. Tell them about your strengths and weaknesses and in what areas you need help to be successful. Tell your boss that you can do your job and tell your partner what you need to be happier. Your world will become more about what you require to be a success.

red and you

THE MORE YOU LIKE RED, the less tolerance you have for failure or incompetence.

THE LESS YOU LIKE RED, the more you will tolerate things that you do not enjoy.

be specific

Get control of your environment or it will control you. What are you doing right now? Exactly what do you need to do? Get out your magnifying glass. Look at each thought and activity that is absorbing your time. Direct your energy towards people and situations that are worth your attention. Others will feel your energy. They will know you are not playing games.

Tell others specifically what you can or can't do. You will become able to do what they expect—a success. If you are not being direct and specific, or if they are stubbornly focused on themselves, they can perceive "facts" about you that are false.

express it ™

say it . . . powerfully!

After 24 years in the human resources field, I met many powerful human resources executives who had the capability to be president or C.E.O of their companies. Yet, they did not get promoted. Their low-key self-presentation was perceived as not being powerful.

Expressing who you are, whether in a personal situation or inside a big company, allows others to know what you can do. If you don't tell them who you are, don't expect them to know. Like it or not, you are going to be perceived as who you say you are. OOPS! Isn't how you are perceived, ultimately, how you perceive yourself? Turn up the volume. Make strong, definite statements.

RED-ORANGE POWER

Red-orange gives you the self-respect to honor your individuality. Respecting yourself starts with appreciating those around you. Honor those who love and respect you, and you will gain the power to honor yourself.

Make time for whoever or whatever is important. Your focused concerns will get things done and show others how much you care. Ask yourself about what or whom you are thinking. Isn't it about what or who is most important to you? If not, get your act together.

red-orange and you

THE MORE YOU LIKE RED-ORANGE, the more you honor your individuality.

THE LESS YOU LIKE RED-ORANGE, the more difficult it is for you to distinguish yourself from society.

make time for what is important

I have had the same housekeeper for over 25 years. She is really famous among my friends for her fried chicken. One day when I asked how she made such incredibly delicious chicken, she replied, "I just know when to take it off the fire." She cared enough to devote her time to watching the fire.

Little children know the importance of time. They know instinctively, the moment they see you, how much you care. Take the time to feel each person's heart. Investing your time to connect with the humanity inside of each person will not reward you every time, but overall it will give back much more love than you gave out.

respect yourself

Ask yourself, "Do those I listen to, listen to me?" "Do those I love, love me?" When you give to someone by thinking about them or being with them, you give them your most valuable gift—your time. You make them important. Are they making you important as well? If not, why continue? Direct your emotions and your time toward those who have authentic concern and love for you.

let your heart lead

So who would you miss? Pretend that the world is coming to an end and that you can only save your family and five other people you care about. Consider who they are.

Now, write or tell each one of them why you care about them. Their sincere appreciation will make you feel important. Your spirit will bask in the ultimate sunshine—love.

ORANGE POWER

Orange makes positive change easier for you. It enables you to disassociate from what you expect from yourself to realize the clarity of a situation. You gain the power to eliminate or change the direction of dead-end situations and relationships.

Be realistic about what you promise or expect. Everyone is happier when you're realistic about what you can and can't do. How long will it take you to finish? Is there enough time? Constantly reevaluate your expectations of yourself and others. When you find yourself working harder or feeling too serious, ask those around you, "How am I doing?"

orange and you

THE MORE YOU LIKE ORANGE, the easier it is for you to disassociate from your expectations to see the truth of a situation.

THE LESS YOU LIKE ORANGE, the more you tend to expect from yourself—more than you can deliver.

do what you say

I overheard a friend in Atlanta telling her aunt that she could be in West Virginia by seven o'clock, in time for dinner. When I asked "How can you drive from Atlanta to West Virginia in eight hours?" she said defensively, "I drive really fast." I insisted we look at the mileage.

We computed that if she drove 120 miles per hour, never stopping to eat or get gas, she would arrive at four o'clock the next morning, instead of at seven in time for dinner. She was about to let her aunt down and fail, no matter how well she performed.

under-promise, over-deliver

Instead of working harder and harder to make a situation or a relationship work, simply ask, "How am I doing?" If you are sincere, they will tell you. A word of caution: If they say, "Everything is fine," and look uncomfortable, ask the same question again.

Acknowledge how long it will take to accomplish each thing that you are going to do, before you promise something. Everyone will be happier, including you, when you tell them what you can and can't do up front. Ha! Why not be marvelous? Promise less than what you believe you can deliver. Okay, now breathe.

GOLD POWER

Gold gives you the power to rediscover what gives you pleasure. Ignite your inner fire. Give yourself time to do what feels good. Play. Your new awareness of exciting people and situations will give you the power to dismiss and eventually discard your undesirable thoughts and situations.

Your new carefree, more passionate perspective will convey confidence and attract friends and business. Always doing what you are supposed to be doing will run your battery down. Do what your heart desires and your energy will zoom.

gold and you

THE MORE YOU LIKE GOLD, the more you know how to use your resources to create new things.

THE LESS YOU LIKE GOLD, the more your undesirable thoughts distract you from knowing what makes you passionate.

play keeps you on track

Listen to the tone of other people's voices. It is easy to hear who is full of passion and who has lost it. Don't become a zombie. If you are constantly doing what you are supposed to do, not what you enjoy, you will lose your spirit as well.

Keep your passions on track by having fun each day. Create the downtime to feel your essence. Only then will you know how you really feel. You will see what makes you passionate and be able to eliminate your undesirable thoughts. Say yes, not no, to the adventure of being alive.

the play game

"Unplan" your day off. In the example below, your day off is Saturday. So, let's begin the night before.

FRIDAY NIGHT AFTER 9:00 PM.
Discard your thoughts on work, watching TV, and serious reading. Turn off your phone and your alarm. Before you go to bed, let your thoughts roam free.

SATURDAY, WHEN YOU AWAKE
Think, "What do I want to do today?" Don't rush. Allow time for just YOU. Take a bath, shower, or go for a walk. Keep it quiet. Avoid playing music or listening to the radio.

You will start to experience a deeper awareness of your desires. Respect these feeling as the source of all your passion.

YELLOW POWER

Yellow gives you the wisdom to know what you need. Constantly critique the ongoing conversation you are having with yourself by reevaluating what you are getting from others and situations. You will gain the power to know what motivates you and see the reality of others.

Listen for the reality of each situation or what each person is motivated to accomplish. Don't waste your time on something you cannot change or someone who doesn't know what they want. Each person or situation is that way for a reason. Accept it as it is and move on to what fits or who will support you the most.

yellow and you

THE MORE YOU LIKE YELLOW, the more willing you are to get information before coming to conclusions.

THE LESS YOU LIKE YELLOW, the sooner you come to a conclusion, even if you have not heard all of the facts.

everyone is doing their own thing

Accept the fact that your thoughts are just about you. Even when you are helping someone, you are doing your own thing. Your contribution is making you feel important. Pay attention. What are you getting from what you do? Listen for what others are getting as well.

Look to your own motivation. If one moment you are intensely concerned with yourself, the next overly concerned with situations or others, be aware. Confess the reason you are doing what you are doing. You will gain the inner peace of knowing the power and limitations of each relationship or situation.

let the sun shine

Your spirit knows only the moment. Gloom can appear to be forever. Accept that gloom is a time to understand yourself and sunshine is a time to express yourself. Together, they make up the process of being human. You need both.

For fun on a rainy day, pretend that it is bright and sunny. Like crazy you will attract others to you. Your high energy will give them the hope to start looking beyond the gloom of the day. After all, a positive thought is the beginning of a new tomorrow.

BLACK POWER

Black gives you the courage to know your emotions. Take the plunge. Feel both your pleasant and painful experiences, but don't obsess over them. You will experience the power of genuine appreciation for yourself and others.

When you don't recognize something, it controls your emotions, and eventually your actions. Thoughts such as, "Everything about that person or a situation is perfect" or "Is life worth living?" are warning signs that you are avoiding a self-truth. Ask friends for their input. Take notes and think hard about their comments every morning when you arise. Your life will have more value.

black and you

THE MORE YOU LIKE BLACK, the more you are ruled by your emotions.

THE LESS YOU LIKE BLACK, the more you avoid your emotions.

be first-class

Give each person you meet a part of you. They will, for the most part, become more human. To "hide" your heart and not relate on a personal level is to be forgotten the minute you leave the room. Look each person in the eye. Say hello with your heart, and good-bye using the person's name. Be first-class; show the world you have style.

Treasure those around you and they will respect you. Always appreciate their contribution. Be sincere. Watch your pronouns. WE creates a union, I is all about you. Isn't class simply honoring the humanity within each person?

your ups and downs

You and the rest of humanity exist in a constant flux of mood swings. Your darker side, your emotions, allow you to feel what you need. Your thoughts, your lighter side, give you the ability to distinguish who or what you want.

Be serious about your life, not yourself. Trust your emotions and surrender your ego. Otherwise, your emotions or frustrations will begin to build. Then you will react. The longer you wait, the more dramatic your reaction will be. Give equal respect to both the light and dark sides of yourself.

"The dark is equally
important as the light."

CHARLOTTE BRONTE

BROWN POWER

Brown grounds you. Immerse yourself in understanding the natural process of life and things. Get to really know a person or situation before you judge it. You will gain the power of awareness, becoming able to embrace life, people, and things as they are.

Be real. Don't get caught up in the rat race or try to gain everyone's approval. Forget about power and status. The more airs you put on and the harder you try to disguise your shortcomings, the more apparent they are for everyone to see. You'll make stronger connections with others by accepting yourself as you are.

brown and you

THE MORE YOU LIKE BROWN, the more aware you are of your environment and the temporary nature of life itself.

THE LESS YOU LIKE BROWN, the longer it takes you to realize the realities of your environment and life itself.

life's greatest lesson

Farmers, the old-fashioned type without fancy irrigation devices, are very grounded. They live a life where a crop planting can be ruined because of lack of rain. Imagine working very hard for months, doing everything right, and coming up with nothing.

Accepting failure, without taking it personally, is life's greatest lesson. People and things just are. Are you grounded in reality? Pay attention to your thoughts. Accept the benefits of your failures. Many uncomfortable situations or relationships teach you great lessons.

the universe is talking to you

Every time you start something without honestly appraising a situation or yourself, you are setting yourself up for a fall. Your arrogance will come back to haunt you. Below are a few examples of butt-biting arrogance.

"I am really attractive"	"I am better than everyone else"	"I know everything"
so...Your need to prove yourself makes you artificial, unattractive.	so...Others see you as a conceited jerk, not of importance to them.	so...You don't listen and know very little.

"Pride goeth before destruction,
and a haughty spirit before a fall."

PROVERBS 16:18

WHITE POWER

White gives you the objectivity to see all of your available options. Step back and view your world as if you were not a part of it. Let your sharpest eye roam into every facet of your life. In keeping your distance, you will gain the power to decipher new opportunities for yourself and those you love.

Being objective allows you to distinguish the possible resources. Ponder this question: In the entire world, if you could have anything, what or who would it be? Now look at each of your current relationships and situations and decide what you need to change, request, keep, or let go.

white and you

THE MORE YOU LIKE WHITE, the faster you are able to shift gears and explore new options.

THE LESS YOU LIKE WHITE, the longer it takes you to break free of problematic situations.

distance creates objectivity

When you get upset or feel uncomfortable, think about the price you are paying for what you want. Take a step back. Be objective. Making your life complicated has more to do with your mindset than your environment. Distance gives clarity. It gives you the control to regain yourself.

your vices and virtues

Your greatest talents and your greatest weaknesses are the same. If you attack your weaknesses, you stand the risk of losing your greatness.

> **"Every vice is only an exaggeration of a necessary and virtuous function."**

> RALPH WALDO EMERSON

With time, however, and an investigative spirit, you can focus on where your virtues end and your vices begin. Being completely objective with yourself will allow you to cut away your vices without sacrificing your virtues.

VICE	VIRTUE
You don't accept other people's views.	You possess a persistent focus.
You finish tasks without knowing all the facts.	You make decisions on time.
You expend a lot of possible energy on unnecessary things.	You eliminate failure. before it occurs.

BE TRUE TO YOURSELF

Keep the power within you by constantly being aware of the nevers. Don't let these obstacles stop you from realizing your self or the world around you. Be true to yourself and respect others by allowing them to do the same.

never force change

If you feel that you are in a rush to change, you are not accepting yourself, someone else, or a situation as it already exists. Change begins with awareness. It gives you the power to better direct and manage your actions.

never generalize

Generalizations are usually inaccurate. When you use words like "always" or "never," be careful. You will lose the ability to see facts. Open up your life to the world around you. Opportunity can exist only if you allow it to.

never disagree at the start

When someone disagrees with you, make an effort to see his or her point of view. Many times you are both right. Use the word "and" more. For example, consider that you could do this and they could do that or you can be this way and they can be that way. Accept that whatever the other person says is okay. Then think about it again. This is a good way to see if what you were disagreeing about is important enough to argue.

never lightly dismiss your defensiveness

Whenever you say, "I do not deserve that" or "I did not do that," you are being defensive. Aren't you just uncomfortable with something about yourself? Stop pushing so hard and the facts will surface. You will be able to focus on what you want. Then tell others what they can expect from you.

never make assumptions

Other people's feelings are not always about you. Are they sad, nervous, or confident? Ask, don't assume. Try to get more information. If you think you know what others are going to say or exactly how a situation will develop, you are not keeping an open mind.

never surround yourself with people who do not believe in or respect you

Real friends listen to how you feel, and even question what you do. When friends fail to point out when you've stepped out of line, they are doing you a disservice. A true friend will ground you in your reality.

never beat yourself up

When you talk down to yourself, little by little you destroy your passion. Emotions should be nurtured, not torn down. To say, "I am fat, old, ugly, stupid, dizzy, or crazy," is destructive. Don't have unrealistic expectations. Give yourself the room to accomplish what you're capable of. You will become a winner.

never try to make your emotions more logical

Your feelings are distinct from your thought processes. Respect your emotions by never questioning them. By separating your heart from your mind, you give both the freedom to breathe. You will actually gain more control. Humor your emotions or you will lose yourself.

never say never

When you say, "I will never love, be hurt, or express that again," you destroy a part of you. You lose a perspective you need and undermine possibilities for your future. When you feel empty or become uncomfortable, be careful. Learn to forgive and forget.

BE YOURSELF

You were born innocent. This childlike quality in you, is YOU. Whenever you put up walls, you lose your pure, passionate spirit. Accept your feelings about the world around you or you will lose sight of the real you. Make your life a passionate journey by trusting your inner voice. Take The Dewey Color System™ Oath.

THE DEWEY COLOR SYSTEM™ OATH

I will trust in my ability to keep my own
energy, and will respect others by allowing
them to go the way they want to go.

Remember when you were a child and you thought you could fly? Well, you were right. Trust your inner self by being yourself. Respect others by allowing them to be who they need to be. Awareness will be your trophy. Your spirit will soar.

trust your intuition

How do you feel right after you walk away from a person or situation? Spend a moment listening to yourself. Are you content, exhilarated, sad, or even depressed? Listen to your inner voice. It is constantly telling you what will bode well for your future.

Surround yourself with exciting people and situations. Their positive energy will give you the strength to stand back and reject what does not work. Admiration is energizing and disgust is debilitating.

Be devoted to respecting the positive people and situations in your life. After a while, you will simply discard the negative. Choose the sunny side and your passions will flourish. You will be able to accomplish anything you desire.

on a final note

Life is like a roller coaster ride. You can choose to take that ride in the dark, not knowing or understanding why you feel or do what you do, or you can "turn on the lights" and really enjoy the experience of life.

My hope is that by reading The Dewey Color System™ you have illuminated the passion and power within you, and that you now know how to give more support to yourself, and those you love.

YOUR LIFE IS PRECIOUS. HONOR YOUR INNER PASSION AND YOUR SPIRIT BY COMMITTING YOURSELF TO CREATING A LIFE WHERE YOU CAN FULLY BE YOURSELF AT HOME, AT WORK, OR WHEREVER YOU GO!

OFFICIAL COLOR PAGE

your color category selections:

CATEGORY	FAVORITE	LEAST FAVORITE
PRIMARY		
SECONDARY		
ACHROMATIC		
INTERMEDIATE		

your color shade selections:

SHADE	1ST FAVORITE	2ND FAVORITE
MENTAL		
PHYSICAL		
SPIRITUAL		
SILENT		

name: _____

OFFICIAL COLOR PAGE

your color category selections:

CATEGORY	FAVORITE	LEAST FAVORITE
PRIMARY		
SECONDARY		
ACHROMATIC		
INTERMEDIATE		

your color shade selections:

SHADE	1ST FAVORITE	2ND FAVORITE
MENTAL		
PHYSICAL		
SPIRITUAL		
SILENT		

name: _____

OFFICIAL COLOR PAGE

your color category selections:

CATEGORY	FAVORITE	LEAST FAVORITE
PRIMARY		
SECONDARY		
ACHROMATIC		
INTERMEDIATE		

your color shade selections:

SHADE	1ST FAVORITE	2ND FAVORITE
MENTAL		
PHYSICAL		
SPIRITUAL		
SILENT		COLOR SYSTEM™

name: _____

OFFICIAL COLOR PAGE

your color category selections:

CATEGORY	FAVORITE	LEAST FAVORITE
PRIMARY		
SECONDARY		
ACHROMATIC		
INTERMEDIATE		

your color shade selections:

SHADE	1ST FAVORITE	2ND FAVORITE
MENTAL		
PHYSICAL		
SPIRITUAL		
SILENT		

name: _____

OFFICIAL COLOR PAGE

your color category selections:

CATEGORY	FAVORITE	LEAST FAVORITE
PRIMARY		
SECONDARY		
ACHROMATIC		
INTERMEDIATE		

your color shade selections:

SHADE	1ST FAVORITE	2ND FAVORITE
MENTAL		
PHYSICAL		
SPIRITUAL		
SILENT		

name: _____

ACKNOWLEDGMENTS

Dewey Sadka, Sr., for his unrelenting faith in my ability.

Jennifer Sipe, my apprentice and creative director, for six years of complete devotion to making this theory a reality.

Roberto Athayde, for exposing me to a world that inspired this creation.

Mary Ann Petro, for her knowledgeable perspectives in decorating.

Queenie Sadka Nassour, for showing me the power of passionate love.

Lillie Mae Sams, for 25 years of love and concern.

My entire staff of Temp Force, for believing in this system and me, especially Debra Drew, John Christian, Ruth Helms, Jill Richards, Dottie Shoop, Monica Evans Lolliecoffer, Dean Morgan, Gloria Thornton, Shirley Miles, Monica Olivier, and Sherry Jenkins.

Ellis Nassour, for his editing insights and for keeping this project on track.

Dr. Brenda Mitchell, for her unselfish guidance.

Graham Fowler of Peachtree Yoga Center, Lee Hammer of The Hammer Clinic, and Cliff Boyce, personal trainer, for their inspiration and support.

CHECK OUT OUR WEB SITE
www.deweycolorsystem.com

Visit our web site and obtain digital passion profiles. You can select printouts for yourself, or e-mail your friends and loved ones with a printout gift. Below find a sample profile list.

CAREER PROFILE: LEARN WHAT MOTIVATES YOU. You will be able to tap into your passions and channel them toward making your career more enjoyable and meaningful.

RELATIONSHIP PROFILE: LEARN HOW OTHER PEOPLE AFFECT YOUR PRIORITIES, NEEDS, CHOICES, FAILURES, AND CONTRIBUTIONS. Understanding how you and those you love relate is bonding. You will gain an appreciation of your contribution and better understand and support your relationships.

EMPOWERMENT PROFILE: EMPOWER YOURSELF BY ALLOWING THE SILENCE WITHIN YOU TO EXIST. Simple knowledge of yourself is empowering. From it comes the confidence to do what you do best.

Order a profile, a copy of The Dewey Color System™ and much more directly off our web site, or write to: Energia®, Inc., 1854 Marietta Blvd., Atlanta, Georgia 30318-2803.

**ENERGÎA
PRESS**
SM **color products available**

THE DEWEY COLOR COORDINATOR™...$24.95

Take this book with you when you're buying clothes or furnishings. At a glance you will see 76 colors that coordinate with your pants, shirts, furniture, and walls. Use this brilliant shopping guide to make your world more spiritual, sensual, and adventurous.

WHAT'S YOUR FAVORITE COLOR?™...$8.95

Give your child the gift of passionate, brilliant color. This interactive children's book for ages 6 months to 8 years will teach your child basic color and reading skills. Use it in conjunction with The Dewey Color System™ to better understand how to be supportive without destroying your child's essence.

THE DEWEY COLOR CARDS™...$1.95 EACH

Use the powerful vibrations of color to open up new perspectives. Select a motivational command from this card collection to express an electrifying thought and color. Inspiration begins with the heart.

THE DEWEY COLOR PUZZLE™...$8.99

Put your color skills to the test. This fun, fast puzzle will challenge your ability to see color. Complete it in under 5 minutes and you are a color hue expert. Practice makes perfect. Do it over and over to sharpen your visual color skills.

for the store nearest you

call 1-866-351-5001 or
log on to our web site: www.deweycolorsystem.com